Mommie Diarist

A Collection

Robyn Lane Books
Coppell, Texas

Mommie Diarist/ Robyn Lane Books. -- 1st ed.
ISBN 978-0-99-06473-5-5

Contents

Foreword

Like so many women, I would tell you that my life did not truly begin until the birth of my son. I had a happy, fulfilling life, but when that baby came into my world, it was like someone changed out my perfectly fine 60-watt for a 100-watt light bulb. Suddenly, everything was brighter. Even sleep deprived with bleeding nipples and a bruised bottom, I was happier than I had ever been.

Brighter light bulbs mean better vision, and better vision meant I could see the good and the bad with more clarity. I cried as much as my baby in those first few months of motherhood. I cried for joy, out of fear and frustration, because of actual physical pain, and for no reason at all. I cried because I was exhausted and overwhelmed, and because I was so full of passion for this tiny, needy human, I thought I would burst.

As Robyn and I began curating the essays for this collection, I was looking for voices to convey all of what I had experienced. I was looking for honesty about the good, the bad, the ugly, and the most beautiful parts of parenting. I wanted to read stories that would make me feel something, stories I could identify with, and stories that would teach me something new.

I believe we succeeded. I have startled the dog by laughing out loud, and I have frightened people in coffee shops by bursting into tears while reading submissions. I have learned and I have grown as I have read these essays, and I have been able to reflect on and better appreciate my experience as a mother and as a daughter.

My mother has given me the gift of unconditional, unwavering love and acceptance, and if I do this parenting thing properly, my son will grow up with the same safety net. My part in this book is rooted in gratitude for the mother I have, and in hope for the mother I am.

Read it and weep, friends. Read it and laugh. Read it and learn. Read it and grow. If you need me, I'll be trying to catch my son, so I can hug him and smell his head.

-Lane

Motherhood makes you crazy. There is no function of life that will make you more certifiably insane. It wasn't until I became a mother that I understood that the insanity is stupefyingly beautiful. This collection of essays is a rounded example of just how beautiful the insanity is.

When organizing a collection of voices that are meant to represent the inner monologue of mothers, the most gratifying element is the diversity of voices you experience while reading submissions. Fortunately, Lane and I had a wealth of words to pull from, and we are giddy with joy over sharing the chosen words with you.

Make a cup of tea, grab some tissues, and get acquainted with these Mothers. At the very least, you will be entertained, if not enlightened, inspired, moved, or touched.

-Robyn

Mommie Diarist

Falling in Love the Last Time
by Virginia Woodruff

I stopped just long enough to buy flowers in the gift shop after flying from my new home in sunny Texas back to foggy California. My mother was in the hospital. Again.

When she was diagnosed with lymphoma, her oncologist had given her the impression that this was a low-level cancer, the kind you lived with. She stuck with that idea despite evidence to the contrary. She called chemotherapy her "therapy" and refused to go to a grief counselor. "It's not for me," she'd say, waving the idea away the same way she turned down spa treatments or Broadway plays.

When I got to her room, the bouquet of flowers I'd bought wasn't allowed in because of germ restrictions to protect her fragile immune system. This denial felt like the first cruelty; if you can't bring a person in the hospital flowers, what can you do?

I had to put on a surgeon's mask to enter the room. "Who'd have thought I'd wind up here," my mother asked when she saw me, as if for a lark she'd checked into a hotel. She'd been fine the day before, but in the night had fallen out of bed and been unable to move. Yes, it was one of those *I've fallen and I can't get up* necklaces that saved her.

I spent that first night in a hard hospital chair, accompanied by beeping machines, having "hallway talks" with eager young doctors. My husband and toddler son were on their way.

My sister conveniently had the "flu" in Vermont. She reminded me that her doctor told her not to fly with clogged sinuses. She was never the one who volunteered for the difficult job. I was on my own, a tourist with no guidebook.

My mother was what you would call an eccentric. A native New Yorker, she reluctantly learned to drive after my father moved her out to the country at age thirty-five, but refused to get on freeways (shutting down my chance at ballet). She was from a different generation than my friends' carefree parents, born in 1928, but waiting to have children until the unusual ages of thirty-five and forty. She once told me she was afraid she wouldn't be a very good mother because her mother had been so distant.

Ideas from the War and the Depression lingered in our country farmhouse and fit well with her straitened circumstances. She recycled everything, washed plastic sandwich bags hung drying like ghosts around our kitchen.

In college, she had been a groupie of John Cage and Merce Cunningham. But she scorned pop culture—Elvis, the Kennedys, and everyone who followed. She loved all things English, which at one point included my father. After his early death, she didn't romanticize him, but she embraced his country as the place where things were done better. She developed a crush on pasty Prime Minister John Major. If you got up at night for a glass of water you would hear the trickle of the overnight BBC broadcast emanating from her room. As a widow, she lived the Jane Austen life centered on tea, cats, books, walks, and hole-y wool sweaters.

Though she gave up her chance at a career, she kept studying; her books were marked with notes and cross-references. In later life she abandoned fiction for non-fiction, specifically history, preferably ancient history. "Nothing interesting happened after 1066," she would say. But this still left room for historical romances, which were stacked alongside Marcus Aurelius and the Stoic philosophers. When my husband mentioned he studied American literature in college, she said, "How can you read that dribble?"

My mother wasn't an easy patient in the hospital. "Do you consider this my side?" she'd ask after the nurses had carefully rotated her once again. Her complaints didn't align with what the doctors were worried about. She was bothered by an incessant cough. They could stick a tube down her nose and drain the fluid, but it would be uncomfortable. Yes, she wanted to do it right away. Each time they came in she asked the nurses to do it again. I felt the awkwardness in the room as I came to understand the more serious complications they were battling, yet for my mother the cough was the only problem.

As the hours went by, her blood pressure dropped. She slept more and went from complaints to grunts to moans when the nurses turned her from side to side. I cringed as she moaned. *Is that really necessary? If she's so sick, why are we worried about bedsores?* But I didn't know if I was allowed to speak up.

My mother tore at her oxygen mask. I remember hating the oxygen mask I needed when I gave birth. It had a nauseating mint smell and I thought it was choking me. So I let her slip it off when the nurses left the room. *Who was I there to please, my mother or the medical staff?* It would have helped if I had known what was at stake.

My mother was starting to look like a different person, smaller, but also younger, as the IV fluids puffed out her skin and filled in her wrinkles. But the nurses weren't looking at her face; they were looking at the screen above her that tracked oxygen levels. Soon I also kept one eye on those numbers as they rose and fell.

My mother had signed a do-not-resuscitate form, but that left a lot of questions unanswered. Should they put in a central line? This would save her from constant needles, but it was a minor surgery. I looked at the doctor's face. He seemed eager. I said yes. I said yes to everything.

I was in that familiar place of not knowing the right thing to do. Other people seemed born or raised with more practical knowledge than me. When it came to many life decisions, I was just guessing. The bigger the decision, the bigger the guess.

Time passed, but it felt like one long day inside the fluorescent fish tank of the hospital. An old friend called my cell phone. *Keep talking*, I willed, *just don't give me the burden of conversation.* At one point she said, "Just know you're not alone," and I cried into the phone. When I had taken the flowers downstairs to return to the gift shop, waves of anger passed through me as I watched people chatting and laughing, going about their lives. Didn't they know my mother was sick upstairs?

The next morning, a brisk oncologist arrived trailing a cold wind. My mother's usual doctor wasn't on call. This oncologist was irritated by what the ICU doctors had accomplished. She gave us a dressing down: forget the surgeons' masks, the central line was unnecessary, as was the oxygen. The cancer had spread to my mother's spinal cord. *That's why she couldn't get up.* Her immune system was shot. My mother's doctor had been a softie for keeping her alive so long with blood transfusions, my mother's beloved treatments. *She means my mom is dying,* I translated to myself. This doctor had no concern that it was the first time I was getting the news.

The rush of comprehension was worse than the medical decisions. *This is how my mother will die. Now. In a hospital.* It felt unjust. I had imagined long deathbed scenes at home, time to reminisce, the way it happens in movies. Insert "Guilt" here, especially since she entered the hospital two weeks after we moved away. Had I taken away her will to live? I was abandoning her after I had gone to the trouble of uprooting her from the East Coast. What was more important: your needy mother or the collapsing California housing market?

I regretted that I didn't say goodbye while she was still able to talk. But I couldn't bring up the subject of death with my mother, even in the ICU. I didn't want to upset her, I didn't want her to give up the fight, but mostly, I knew she wanted to stay in denial and keep her privacy. "This is just another treatment," she would have said.

The oncologist turned to my mother and announced, too loudly, "We're going to baby you." My mother groaned in acknowledgment. I was embarrassed. I shouldn't be witnessing this. I was also offended: how dare she insult my intelligent mother with her baby talk?

They transferred us to a quiet room at the end of a long hallway, the hospital's answer to hospice. It had a mini refrigerator and a beige sleeper-sofa, but it was nobody's home. A morphine drip stood stoically by the bed. Suddenly there was nothing to do. My mother lay tucked in and tilted up. Her eyes were closed, and she was breathing like the real yogis do–long sucking breath in, infinite pause, long breath out. It wasn't that she was trying to catch her breath so much as the process of breath was extending.

When the nurse asked me if she should send someone in, I was tempted to pick a religion at random. I longed for a ritual to tell me what to do. But we were not religious, and it would have felt hypocritical to ask for help now. I felt my mother's pride. There would be no minister with a calm hand on the head, no rabbi reciting ancient prayers. And I had nothing to replace them with.

The next day a social worker appeared and gave me a pamphlet. Here were facts, however general, that I could cling to. Apparently hearing is the last sense to go, so you should talk to the dying.

I reverted to my newly acquired mothering skills. To

help my son fall asleep, I would recount his day back to him while rubbing his back. Now I narrated my mother's life to her as best as I could. I told her about her childhood summers on Long Island, the ones she'd said had saved her. Did she remember the dogs her mother would get? I left out the part where her mother returned the dogs to the pound at summer's end. Remember when you were caring for two little girls? You said those were your favorite years.

My husband arrived with our toddler. My son, never one for boundaries, clambered onto the bed and touched the bruises on my mother's hand where nurses had tried to insert IV's. "Ouchie," he said. They left to get a hotel room where my son could burn off energy in a pool.

I filled a CD player with my mother's favorite composer, Handel. I bought a copy of *Pride and Prejudice*. A lifelong insomniac, my mother would often ask me to read her to sleep, so I read about Elizabeth Bennet's marital prospects until it felt ridiculous, given the setting.

Then, insert "Guilt" again, I went shopping. It was cooler in California than I had expected and I wanted a sweater. Or maybe it was that old instinct: when you don't know what to do, go shopping. I went to the same department store where I had taken my mother many times. I pictured her there, refusing my suggestions and insisting her threadbare clothes were just fine.

When I returned to the hospital room, it took me a minute to realize that my mother's long breaths had stopped. Everything else was the same. I touched her shoulder; it was still warm. I stood there next to the bed. I couldn't take my hand off her. Those minutes were long and quiet, and unexpectedly undramatic. Finally, I walked down the hall to tell the nurse.

A month later, I walked through the bicoastal memorial services she hadn't wanted. She didn't like the idea of people talking about her. Those who knew my mother spoke about their version of her, usually a caricature. I studied the pictures of her in crisp wool suits as a college student. Had her life turned out as she'd hoped? There were matters to attend to: selling the house, sorting the things. It keeps you busy.

But when I was finally settled in our new home, sleep became more difficult. Now the image of my dead mother lying in the hospital bed, eyes closed and mouth open, revisited me as a haunting memory. I didn't want to close my eyes.

Then I had a dream. My mother and I were sitting on the dock of a bay (yes, cheesily enough, just like the song), our feet skimming the top of the water, the sounds of waves surrounding us. My mother said I could sell her house, but I should be sure to throw in a case of beer for the new owners.

I don't know whether this was a wish fulfillment or some random assembly of images from my brain, but the dream released me. And her house from the squabble my sister and I were having. I still shielded the wound, but publicly I could talk about my mother's death as just another event on the timeline. We had a baby, we sold our house, we moved, my mother died, my son started preschool.

    Despite my atheism, I'd followed the path many religions describe: a restless period of fear followed by a peaceful period of remembrance. Perhaps this is the natural arc we all go through as we wrestle with the incomprehensibility of death, especially when it's our parents'. Why my interpretation involved a case of beer I'll never know.

    When I talk about her death to my son—and now also to my twin daughters—I wish I could mention heaven. But I've found an honest way to tie up the narrative. I say that my mother lives on every day I take care of them because she taught me how to do it. If her biggest achievement was to overcome an under-loved childhood, it was more than enough.

    Losing a parent is one of those fogged-in experiences you can't really know until you get there, like having a child. In the same way I connect with other mothers now, I also feel an immediate bond with strangers who have lost their parents: adult orphans. There's a lot you don't have say. That you think about your mother every day. That you're unsympathetic when friends cry over losing grandparents. And there's the unmentionable fact that you might be happier and braver now that there's no one to report back to, or that you get along with your sibling better now that there's no one to win a gold star from.

    I miss the person she was, never to be replicated. I miss the history of the family, the need for hand-written thank you notes. I miss the safety, the person I could call when I was sobbing and snotty, the lap where I would lay my head as a child. When my friend's mother died, I told her the one thing I've learned: the world's a different place without your mother in it.

Virginia Woodruff founded the website Great Moments in Parenting, where parents share the agony and the ecstasy of life with kids. She's working on a book about motherhood, how it's changed from our mothers' generation, and why it's harder today. She lives with her husband and three children in Austin, TX.

Be Prepared: A Letter from Your Future Self
by Emily Reese

Hello Darling. Don't you look wonderful, all young and carefree? Yes, this is you from the future. No, we will not be discussing how this is possible or the space-time continuum this evening. We have more important business. You, dear girl, are going to be a mother.

It won't be today, but it is coming. They are coming. It's time to get you prepared.

First things first: you most likely won't fail. How do I know? You're reading this, aren't you? That proves you possess the two-shit minimum you are required to give to be a halfway decent parent.

Good on you.

Next, I want you to take a look at yourself. You are fucking beautiful. You are not too tall/short/fat/skinny/pale/tan/whatever you seem to think you are. In fact, you are so damn wonderful that you are going to decide to make little duplicates of yourself, with help from another person.

Right now I want you to do something for me. Go stand in front of a mirror. Now turn around. Look back over your shoulder and give your reflection a saucy wink. See? That's what I'm talking about.

Why all the self love, you ask? Because, my sweet self, you are sadly getting close to your superficial hotness peak. Society is all about the young and beautiful (You Now), not the tired, messy-haired, frazzled, Queen of the Yoga Pants, Super Mom you will someday become.

How can Super-messy-yoga-pants be a good thing? To begin with, she is a badass.

This woman you will become can conquer anything. Remember how gross poo is? Like, how you nearly had a panic attack that one time a bird pooped on your head? That bird ain't got nothin' on the poo that's coming for you. Not only that, but the "little angels" that "bless" you with said poo will someday delight in telling strangers about your bird poop freak out. They think that story is hilarious.

Not only that, but one day, you will catch vomit. Not because you have to, but because you just changed that little monster and you're running out of clean onesies and bibs.

And after that, you will shrug it off. Then you will strut around in your yoga pants, because you are one bad mamma jamma.

This woman does not leap tall buildings in a single bound. That's for wusses. This woman will grow entire human beings with her body. Not only can she make actual people, she can do it while continuing her normal routines.

What's that, Batman? No, you can't do that shit. Damn straight.

When you are this woman, your senses will take on new, highly effective levels. Drool has a smell. You will wear it like a fine perfume if that's what it takes to calm one of your progeny when they're sick. You will instantly recognize that look a toddler gives you right before running towards the street. That "Ready to race, Mommy?" look. Your super hearing is going to be so extraordinary, you will be able to distinguish the difference between a hurt cry and a pissy cry and will instantly become aware of the foreboding sound of silence. Whilst incubating your tiny humans, your favorite foods will suddenly taste like shit, while things you never like before become ambrosia. Your fingertips can magically tell the difference between a rash, a bug bite, and "Dear God, what is that?" This isn't a cruel twist of fate; this is how you get everything you need to grow a person without even trying.

Take that Superman. (He doesn't know, either.)

Someday, when you become me, you're going to delight in things that make absolutely no sense to you now.

There will be the first time your baby smiles at you. It's about as close to gratitude as an infant can get, and it is awesome.

Or you will be whistling to your toddler and they will stick a chubby finger in your mouth trying to touch the sound. Silly baby.

When they're older, you will find yourself spontaneously singing the Screaming Goat version of a song together in the car. (It's a thing, trust me.)

You will, at bare minimum, wax nostalgic on the first day of school. You will enjoy packing lunches and leaving tiny notes inside. You will look at them, and see a future life-long friend.

You will stress out about millions of things. Here's a few we've done that I can tell you about:

- Babies are surprisingly resilient. They bend and bounce and everything -- just don't abuse it.
- Breastfeeding doesn't come easy to everyone. If you can rock it, great. If not, that does not automatically count as a parenting fail.
- Speaking of fails, try to get those out of the way early as much as you can. They won't remember anything from before three years of age.
- At some point, you will lick food off your child's head. It happens in the animal kingdom all the time. It's really no big deal.
- You can 100%, absolutely do this on your own. That being said, like most things, it's easier with a partner.
- Just because your mother/sister/grandmother/aunt/best friend/arch nemesis excelled at any of this does not mean you will. Nothing is guaranteed. Try not to hate those who have it easier, and give gratuitous sympathy to those who are worse off. (No, honey, we never did get the boobs we wanted. I know. I'm still pissed, too.)
- You're going to call and apologize to your parents. Frequently. Most of the time, they will be gracious about it.
- Everyone is going to have an opinion on what the

"right" way is, when it comes to parenting. They
didn't create your child. You did. Take the advice
with a grain of salt. And try to refrain from telling
them to fuck off.

- Your little spawnlings will say or do something
  someday to embarrass you. It's inevitable. The
  good news is, you have their teenage years to make
  it up to them.

Now, before you go off gallivanting at a bar,
flaunting that cute little wink we did earlier, I need to leave
you with a few parting thoughts. At some point during your
first pregnancy, you may have a "why the hell did I think
this was a good idea?" moment. Yes, during the morning
sickness and water retention, it may seem like you've been
taken over by a parasite. You may fear losing yourself to
this thing called motherhood. And when you finally meet
them, it may not be love at first sight; there's a whole lot
going on when a baby is delivered, and your body is trying
not to go into shock. It's okay. I repeat, it's okay.

In no time at all, you will be all about that little
snuggle bug, saying things in voices that would make the
You Now want to vomit. Speaking of which, Young Us aka
You Now never dies. You're still here with me right now,
albeit rolling your eyes at me because we actually got to
stay up this late, and we didn't even take the time to enjoy
a glass of wine. (You're right. I'll do better next time.)

Scared yet? Don't be. I told you. We are Super Mom. We've got this. Now go out and shake what our mama gave you... for the both of us.

Emily Reese has a degree in Communications. She resides in Ft. Worth, Texas with her husband, 5-year-old daughter and newborn daughter, her pug, and two cats. Her novel Second Death is now available. She is currently working on her follow-up in the series, Second Life.

Sun and Moon
by Meredith McGee

My mother says that when she got her first period I was suddenly just "there," sort of tap-tapping on her shoulder, letting her know that I wanted to get onto the planet. I guess I had awhile to wait because she didn't have me until she was twenty-four. The midwife who delivered me said I was born smiling and just batting my eyelashes, and it was clear that I was happy to be here. That wasn't so much the case for my brother, who was born 5 years later, almost to the day (and to my stepdad, my parents having divorced), but with lots of reluctance and struggle.

As children, we were in awe of our mother. She was beautiful and witty and smart and people were drawn to her and revolved around her like she was a movie star. She expected us to be smart, too. She never spoke in baby talk to us or to her other children who would come later. She spoke to us like we were just cute, short people who could understand anything and deserved explanation and truth about pretty much everything.

My mother was an amazing cook. We had family dinner around the table every night, and we learned about good food. She hung a chalkboard behind the table and would write words for us to learn or math problems to solve or rhymes and poems because we loved to play word games. So we'd eat and learn and be engaged as a family. She was from Detroit and loved Motown, so sometimes there would be music and she would sing and dance and so would we.

My stepdad was crazy about her. My brother and I were crazy about her. But at times it seemed like she'd go off into her own world. This happened more after my mom went back to school to get a nursing degree. She was gone more. She would closet herself in her room to study. She worked night shifts at the hospital. She slept late because she was tired. She went out with new friends that she'd met in school. Things were changing and our parents didn't seem as happy. It made the time we did spend together even more precious. Over the years, I've said many times that my mother was like the sun. She shone very brightly and when she was focused on you it was like being in the warmest light. But when she didn't, it was like being in the dark and cold.

Our family's winter began when my mom took an extended trip to West Texas. She had to get some things sorted out in herself, and she felt a connection to a particular place that might enable her to do that. It was a ghost town in the desert close to Mexico.

I wasn't doing so well. My seventh grade year had gone up in flames when I experienced the trauma of becoming a social pariah, thanks to the lies of a group of boys and the subsequent shaming by my peers at school. I moved in with my dad. This served the purpose of allowing me a new start in a new district and removing me from what seemed to be my other family's turmoil.

I went back all the time. I loved my brother and my stepdad and wanted to spend time with them. I felt responsible for both of them in my mother's absence. My mom would come back and visit, and a couple of times we went to see her, I think. I remember my stepdad putting us on a train to West Texas and giving me a letter to deliver to my mother. The train was freezing. My brother and I huddled together for the eight-hour trip, while condensation dripped a slow patter on us from the vent above. It was miserable.

Sometime after that trip, my mom came for a few days. She and my stepdad took us to dinner at a pizza place downtown and told us they were getting a divorce. My stepdad kept trying to hold her hand. She kept dodging his. Before we left, my brother and I sat on the front steps of the building and I held him on my lap, even though he was too big for that. I think it might have been more for me than him.

Their divorce meant more than just the fracture of our family; it meant she was gone for good and not coming back. Not only that, there was never any mention of my brother or I going to live with her. She had officially left us.

It's not like we never saw her. We went during the summers and stayed for a week. She came to town for weekends here and there. And during those times, it was mostly like the sun was shining again, with the occasional shadow of a boyfriend cast on the time we had together.

Back home, things still weren't going so well. I wasn't getting along very well in my dad's house. I was retreating into depression and anger and the void of abandonment. Dark makeup, dark clothes, dark thoughts and feelings. My dad and stepmom had the good judgment to put me into counseling, where I was able to sort through some of the mess in my heart.

At one point, my counselor encouraged me to tell my mom how angry I was with her, and amazingly I did that during a phone call one evening. I don't remember much of what she said, but I do remember that she listened and didn't tell me I shouldn't feel that way.

There was another evening during that period when I had a memorable phone call with my mother. It was during the first Gulf War. I remember sitting on the counter in my dad's kitchen, and it was mostly dark. While I talked to my mom the TV was on low with images of rockets and tanks and desert in the background.

She said she had been in a fight with her boyfriend, and that he had hit her. It happened outside a joint where they'd been to hear music, and some of the musicians who were friends of hers ran out and restrained him. Ultimately, they ran him out of town. Mom said she was coming to stay for a while and that she needed to be around people who loved her. I said something like, "that's good, I love you," and hung up the phone.

I was shocked. Someone had dared hit my mother? In the way of children, I thought my mother was untouchable. Who could even reach her up there on the pedestal I'd built for her? I hated him passionately and suddenly. And then I got mad at her. Who was she to come back whenever she felt like it because she needed to be loved? Didn't my brother and I need to be loved? Didn't we need her to shelter us and tell us we were good and smart and worthy? But we couldn't get that whenever we felt like it. We had to wait for her to choose to come give it to us.

She did come back. And I'm sure I was glad to see her. I don't remember anything about that visit except that she stayed with her friend, Abby, and fell in love with Abby's roommate. And then they got married and had a kid.

Meanwhile, my relationship with my dad and stepmom had deteriorated to angry silences when I was home, which was mostly never. I met a boy, who happened to be the brother of one of my girlfriends in my therapy group, and I fell in love with him. He was older, 19, and I spent most of my time with him. My dad gave me an ultimatum: shape up or ship out. So I shipped. I moved in with my boyfriend, and we got an apartment. My dad and stepmom emancipated me, and that was it. I was on my own.

My mom's husband had taken a job with IBM, and, at about the same time I was leaving home, she was moving back to town for his contract. She likes to brag about winning the Betty Crocker Good Housekeeping award in high school, and I have to say, she knows how to make a nice home. So it was pretty awesome when she took me shopping to set up my kitchen in that first apartment. She taught me what staples I needed to keep in the pantry to make real food and what tools I needed to use. She wasn't mad at me or disappointed in my situation, she was just very matter-of-fact about the laundry list of things I needed to do to get going.

She and her husband were here for a year or so. My boyfriend and I went frequently to her house for dinner. I loved sitting at her table once more, being fed by my mother, and I loved bonding with my new little brother. And then she was gone again. Back to West Texas, back to the mountains and desert, and this time she had taken my sibling. She had another baby out there, and then there were two little boys. Not long after that, at nineteen, I got pregnant myself.

It wasn't intentional. As a matter of fact, my then-fiancé and I had been fighting so much that I was sure we were on the verge of a break-up. Nevertheless, I knew the moment it happened. I had this overwhelming sense of someone else in the room. Suddenly it made a lot more sense, the tap-tap-tapping my mother had told me about. And so instead of breaking up, my fiancé and I got married.

There was never any question whether I'd keep the baby. I had known my whole life that I'd be a good mother. And I wasn't scared. Before my mom's career as a nurse, she'd been a midwife, and baby-having was just part of women's lives and nothing to be worried about. So I had my baby. What I wasn't prepared for was the excruciating love I could feel for another human being and how that kind of love can strip away whatever peace you've made with your feelings about your own parents.

Slowly, I began to feel angry with my mother again. I didn't understand how anyone who had a child could feel love of that magnitude and ever be able to leave the child willingly. This led me to the conclusion that she simply must not have loved me the way I loved my daughter, which made me wonder what it was about me that was not worthy of that much love. I went round and round in my head with it.

Sometimes my mom would come to town and bring my little brothers. She would always have things she needed to accomplish in the city that she couldn't get done in the ghost town in the desert. So she'd leave the boys with me. Sometimes I'd look at them and wonder if one day she'd feel lost or fed up with her life the way it was and somehow I'd end up raising them. Sometimes, despite loving the boys, I wondered why my brother and I weren't enough for her and she had to go and have two more kids.

And then just as slowly as it had come on, the anger began to ebb. The sharp edges around my love for my daughter softened out into something more malleable and forgiving. Perhaps this had to do with the discovery that motherhood spares no one. I was *being* a mother. And in the being, I was mistaking. And after the mistaking, I was having to learn to forgive myself.

By the time my mother left our family, she had far out-mothered her mother. Her father died in a drunken car accident when she was ten and left his ex-wife no means to support their three children. Impoverished, they hobbled along under my mentally unstable grandmother's minimal care until my mother, being mostly self-sufficient, left home at age fifteen.

She says that when she left, she didn't take us with her because she didn't want to uproot us from our other family members and support systems. She thought we'd be better off where we were, and it had nothing to do with not wanting us with her. She says that if she had known how it would all play out, she would have taken us. And I believe her. When I try to see through the lens of her experience, a woman who had no family behind her and made her own way at fifteen, of course we were better off with our fathers, who loved us and could provide for us. And because she was done being a child long before most children, she must have thought us closer to grown up than we actually were, as well. She nursed us and loved us and fed us and taught us and then when she had to go figure out whatever it was that needed figuring, of course she thought that with solid foundations underneath us, we'd be alright.

My mom and I both divorced our husbands. We both spent long periods as single mothers, with ex-husbands who contributed scantily in some ways to the raising of their children. There were times when I'd be three days from a paycheck and two days away from running out of propane. She'd always help me out of a bind, even though she was on a tight budget herself. If it was groceries or birthdays or a doctor bill, she never wanted me to struggle.

She'd bring the boys to my house a few weekends a year and we'd all be together, and every time her truck pulled out of my driveway, I'd get a lump in my throat and my chest would get tight and I'd miss her even if I could still see her car.

About seven years ago, my brothers asked my mom to move to a bigger city. They were bright, talented children in a narrow and limiting world. So she agreed. Leaving the boys with friends in their old town, my mom got a job an hour from my house and moved in with me while she looked for a house of her own.

She lived with me for about four months. At first, it made me a little crazy. She would move stuff around or leave glasses and Kleenexes all over. She would question why I was doing something a certain way, or tell me the way she would have done it. I'd forgotten what it was like to live with a mother. But we settled into a routine. We'd come home from work, have a glass of wine while my daughter played outside, cook supper, watch TV or play cards, and go to bed. I'd see her in her slippers, the same style she wore when I was a kid, and I'd see the circles under her eyes from the kind of tired that it takes years to build up. I saw her as my friend. Another tired mom.

She did find a house. In a town two hours away. She got the boys ready to move, and then she packed up what little she'd had at my house. And when she pulled out of my driveway that time, with her truck full of clothes and small furniture, I felt like I was thirteen again and my heart was breaking.

Two hours is a lot better than eight. It is easy to see my mom now, and she comes to see me and my kids all the time. The little boys are grown and away at college, and my firstborn will graduate high school soon.

When I was a girl, occasionally my dad would say, "You sound just like your mother." And I knew he was not complimenting me. After my first daughter was born, my ex-husband would say, "You're going to be just like your mother," when we argued. He knew I was afraid that somewhere deep inside of me I had the "leaving gene," and would use that to hurt me. When I remarried and had my second daughter, my husband would say, "You sound just like your mother," and he meant it as if it were a marvel, because I *did* sound just like her.

We spoke to my new daughter in exactly the same way – no baby talk. And I realize now that I speak to my elder daughter the way my mother spoke to me when I was a teenager: matter-of-factly and with no bullshit. In so many ways, I am just like her. I'm strong and independent, proud and vain, generous and liberal, and I laugh loud and long in public. And I know how to make a good home.

Sometimes I feel like I'm high above our lives and the intersections we've made, and when I look down I can see this blur, like a scar, that was that time when she left us to go to the desert. But it's not painful anymore; it's just a remnant of what happened. I wouldn't change it because I wouldn't be who I am had it never happened.

Now my mother sits at my table and we eat food we've prepared together. We sit on my sofa and drink wine and laugh and we sing and dance in my kitchen with my kids. And what was true the day I was born is still true today: I am happy to be here. I chose wisely.

My mom is the Madonna, she is Marilyn Monroe, she is Mother Theresa, she is Kali the Destroyer. We are just two people sharing love and healing karma. She was my first sun, and I am her moon, circling around her star, reflecting the light she gives me back to her.

Meredith is a full-time mother and a part-time writer who can be found "keeping it weird" in beautiful Austin, Texas. She is an avid cook, gardener, and knitter and is good at doing at least one of those things. She's passionate about children with special needs and women's issues and writes about those topics, among others, at her blog http://unchartedwatersmom.com/.

Pursuing Your Passions
While Raising Little People
by Dona Hightower Perkins

"Whenever you see me somewhere succeeding in one area of my life, that almost certainly means I am failing in another area of my life."
    – Shonda Rhimes, Dartmouth commencement speech, June 2014

There is a saying, and I'm not sure who to attribute it to, but it goes along the lines of "You can have it all, just not all at the same time." This is no truer than when it relates to motherhood. Time and age may dictate when you get pregnant and give birth, so everything else has to fall in line with that, whether you like it or not. You may have been born an artist, but childbearing has a definite window of opportunity. The challenge arises when you try to keep your creative side alive but those babies need to be fed, changed, burped, and rocked back to sleep. They don't care that you haven't had a chance to spend time with your muse. In fact, I think they would prefer to projectile-vomit all over your muse so you aren't as easily distracted from the task at hand: taking care of them. Raising children and maintaining your creative life can sometimes make difficult bedfellows.

It was very difficult for me to figure out motherhood and how to get my creative groove back. It has been ten years, in fact. I am just now figuring out what I truly need in order to be creative and what kind of tradeoffs I need to make it happen. Currently the majority of my day is spent with working and mothering and/or household duties. Washing, cooking, cleaning, and so on can take up days at a time if you don't walk away from the mess on occasion. These days when I may only have an hour to spend at the sewing machine or at my computer writing, I have to put my figurative blinders on to the rest of the world/house and block it all out. Every single dust bunny *must* be ignored in order to feed the creative demons. You get better at it with practice and time.

I am 44 years old and I have a 10-year-old son and an 8-year-old daughter. The last 10 years have been a roller coaster ride – lots of highs and lows, ups and downs, perfect moments and missteps. This is motherhood. The frustration set in not because everyone was hungry or needed clean clothes, but because I was awful at prioritizing my own creative needs – it was easier to wash clothes than it was to sit down and write. Yes, there are 24 hours in each day. Yes, I should be able to set aside some time for my creative pursuits. J.K. Rowling did it divorced and in relative poverty. Shirley Jackson did it while raising four kids, later turning her experiences into the delightful book "Life Among the Savages." Danielle Steel juggled three to five books a year while raising nine children and sometimes working three jobs simultaneously, while only sleeping four hours a night. With all the "modern conveniences" we have now, why is it so difficult to carve out an hour for our own creative needs?

Here are five things I have had to learn how to do differently since having kids:

1. The thinking and planning must be done in quiet; the execution can be done in chaos.
2. Never be without pen and paper, sketchbook, etc.
3. Never belittle or ignore your own needs.
4. There will never, ever be enough time for everything you want to do in one day.
5. Learn how to work around the procrastination bug.

I'm in a good place right now; it hasn't always been this way. I was thrilled when I had my first baby in 2003, but there was a time during the first year that I wondered what the hell did I do and how am I going to manage this kid who never seems to sleep and is always wanting something from me? I was not at all prepared for the utter dependency that newborns have on you for their very survival.

I was good at project management. I liked to manage things. I tried really hard to "manage" my baby much like a work project at the beginning. Scheduled feedings, diaper changes, baths. It worked for producing a textbook or writing an article. Why wouldn't it work for raising a human being, too? I guess you could say that I learned the hard way how to be a mother.

Motherhood was a double-edged sword for me, which is something that is not ever mentioned in the pregnancy books or websites that you obsess over as a pregnant lady. Bittersweet, so very joyful and exhausting, the initial hours and days of motherhood are filled with emotion and adrenaline and highs and lows. You desperately wanted this baby, but your life is forever changed. Screaming for hours on end? Your pulse races and you panic, trying anything and everything to fix it. First real smile at mama? Your heart melts. Six weeks after birth your hormones are all over the place, sleep deprivation has set in, and sometimes you find yourself at the bottom of a very dark and very lonely hole.

I feel as if I spent the first year of my son's life in that hole. I didn't know it at the time that I was in such a dark place. I thought it was normal and that everyone had as much trouble as I did adjusting to their new responsibilities and roles and challenges. Doesn't everyone search for a bucket late at night to drown their crying baby in? It was 3AM and no, I didn't do it! I put him back in his crib, shut the door, and turned off the baby monitor instead. There is no law that says you have to keep your baby monitor on all the time.

It wasn't until I joined a moms' group that I realized what a horrible transition it had been for me. I only made it through because of the amazing support system I had in my husband and my mom. I don't care if your support system consists of friends, family members, neighbors, in-laws, gay uncles, or hired help, but get yourself a support system. Your support system should be there when you are close to having a nervous breakdown, people who love and understand you and won't judge your need to take a shower and get away from it all every now and again.

Part of the difficulty with transitioning from independent, self-employed freelancer to mommy was that I had been a workaholic who worked at home long before I got married and had kids. I was used to setting my own hours, managing my own projects, meeting deadlines, and being extremely organized and tidy. I had assumed that my life would continue as it had. The baby could be scheduled into my day just like a phone call so that I could continue to work during naptimes and other times that the baby was occupied. Here's the thing though...babies can't curl up with a good book and read for two to three hours at a stretch. They can't be distracted with TV or video games like older kids can be. You have to *attend* to them and their needs, which really did a number on my orderly, overly scheduled life.

I had to step away from my freelance work for a while, especially after my son started walking at nine and half months old and needed constant supervision. He was a happy, curious little imp, full of life and laughter and movement. Constant movement. It was hard for me – the one who really likes to curl up with a good book – to be so active and always one step ahead. After he started walking, I joined a moms' group, which literally saved my life. There, I was able to see that my normal was normal, and that there were many different types and styles of mothers and children.

I was able to go out for a few "moms only" events, which made me feel like a real person again. I also began to see a counselor, who helped me through many of the anxiety issues I'd been having since giving birth. Like any other job you take on, you must have the right set of tools at the ready for your foray into motherhood. You can't do it alone. It really does take a village. You can't expect your life to ever be the same again; it won't be. It will be better than before, I promise.

Now that my babies are eight and ten years old, I can see that the hole I was in was a serious case of postpartum depression and that I needed to be equipped with the right tools in order to cope. By the time my daughter was born two and a half years later after my son, I was still tired and struggling to get my work done, but I had also learned more about postpartum depression and how to avoid it, how to manage on little sleep, and why babies are God's way of forcing you to stop and smell the roses.

I stopped working briefly after my daughter was born so that I could find my footing again before trying to juggle a newborn, a toddler, and working. When my daughter was six weeks old, I enrolled her and my son in a Mother's Day Out program for two days a week. Best decision I ever made for my family. It gave my son some structured activities and other little ones to play with because he was a busy little bee. My daughter was a hit in the baby room and was loved on and cared for by other sweet mamas. This schedule helped form my New Normal and allowed all of us some breathing room from each other.

I could get some work done on those two days and feel more accomplished, my kids had a chance to have new experiences and friends, and we were all much happier and more content as a family.

As life-changing as it was, I am grateful to have had a chance to have a glimpse into both worlds: stay-at-home mom and work-at-home mom. These experiences helped me grow as a person and challenged me to be a better mom and wife. The schedule that worked so well for us at Mother's Day Out is one I still use to this day. I continue to work from home; freelancing is my passion and my imperative. My house is messy, overflowing with laundry and papers and dishes and unfinished craft projects, but I get a few precious hours by myself to work five days a week. My kids get all of me at 3 o'clock each day for snacks, homework, and the occasional ice cream cone. I get the privilege of tucking them in bed each night. It took almost ten years to get to this point, and I'm thrilled to be here. The point is do what you have to do to find your "happy place" as a mother, whether that is working full-time, staying at home, or somewhere in between.

Dona Hightower Perkins is a redheaded, bespectacled mom of two (Robert, 11 and Isabel, 8), wife of an absent-minded-professor-turned-computer-geek, and doggie mom to three dogs. She loves to write and read and makes a living as a professional writer and editor.

Joshua David
by Gina Curvin

I fell in love with a boy in the 11th grade. Well, it probably wasn't love, but it was a crush of the deepest kind. I knew very little bit about him. We shared one class together, and I only knew his name. I watched him with perfect peripheral vision, as he watched me. I could see he was shy, but I sensed that he might be interested in me, too. I arranged to leave class when he did, searching my brain for reasons to talk with him. We would, but rarely more than a sentence or two.

He was beautiful to me, with the eyes the color of the Caribbean. Strong shoulders that screamed of paddling up and down the California coast. His hair was this beautiful sun-bleached shade of golden brown, and he had this almost Romanesque profile.

One day, he simply disappeared. Stopped coming to class. I didn't see him in the hallways. I stopped thinking about him as much. Stopped hoping I would run into him.

During my senior year, I found out that I wasn't going to have enough credits to graduate with my class, unless I transferred to a continuation high school. The idea terrified me with thoughts of violent and unruly students. Fortunately, I found that most of the kids who attended the continuation school were pretty ordinary, run-of-the-mill kids who, like me, needed to make up units.

I wasn't there very long before a glimpse of that auburn, bleached shoulder-length hair caught my eye and my pulse quickened to that of hummingbird speed. I realized the boon of all boons, the answer to my prayers, he was also a student attending the school.

One day, as I walked home from school, a small two-seater pulled up to me, and a voice asked me if I wanted a ride home. I recognized the voice and quickly said yes, only to wonder how I would fit into such a small car. His friend motioned for me to sit in his lap. I balanced my 110 lb frame precariously, trying with all my might to hold myself up so that his friend would not report back that I was, of all things, fat.

After that, from time to time, he and the friend would offer me a lift, and although we talked briefly, it sent me to the moon and back. A heroin high couldn't have felt as good as time with this boy did.

Eventually, he started to drive me home alone. He was sweet. Never made a move, and to be honest I wasn't sure if he was romantically interested. I wasn't used to a boy like this. I moved with faster, older boys, and was used to being kissed or groped immediately. Here, we shared conversations. He took me to his favorite pizza place. He fixed my means of transportation, a shiny red moped, and I tooled around the beach with him on the back of it.

A few weeks later, while we were playing pool at a friend's house, he leaned into me and gave me the sweetest, softest kiss and asked me to be his girlfriend. I was in teenage ecstasy. We were inseparable from that point on. Early morning surf trips up and down the Southern California coastline and parts of Mexico took up most of our time, where I sat in his oversized hooded sweatshirt, knees tucked up high, bundled until the sun rose and I could make him out, sitting tall and handsome on his board.

I wasn't a virgin when I met him, but we were both naive about birth control. We never discussed the issue, probably both hoping that we were playing the better odds thru sheer denial and silence.

One of his surf trips took him away for a week. Soon after he returned, gossip and mis-communication quietly and quickly tore things apart between us. The break-up was earth shattering, but in my pain, I stood silent and firm holding onto my pride, refusing to question anything. Instead I took my broken heart and finished up the few weeks left of our senior year.

When I missed my first period, I thought nothing of it. Stress. Graduation. The Unspoken Break-Up. It all added up. But soon, reality was tapping at my door. I drew my eyes shut tight. I refused to look at anything except denial.

I have always been the perfect candidate for complete and utter denial. I can physically swallow it down. Those last few weeks of school, I woke up each morning with a sickness that was part heart-break, part dread that something wasn't right, and a small dose of undiagnosed morning sickness. I put my best face forward though because I had a graduation to attend. I had an 18th birthday to look forward to.

The truth here was simple. I was pregnant.

Graduation, birthday, time just marched on. Two weeks after I turned 18, I had a blow-out over curfew with my mother and, in a huff of independence, I stormed out. I ended up at a friend's home that was less stable than my own and lived on her couch until she said enough was enough, and that there simply wasn't enough room for everyone.

By now, the pregnancy wasn't deniable. I wasn't showing, but I wasn't hiding either. I just needed time, time to figure out what I was going to do. I ended up at a friend of a friend's house. She needed a roommate, and I needed a place to live. It was wretched. Drug-addled people showing up all the time. The smell of PCP hung in the air, from time to time. The roommate would stay up sometimes three days running, high on Meth. But I had a roof. My mother and I still hadn't spoken since the day I stormed out.

I finally faced up to the reality of the body living inside of me. I decided on a quiet abortion. I rode the bus into the sketchier part of town and sat with all the other women whose eyes were dull and lifeless. Some scared. One by one, we would be called in for vitals and information, until soon, we didn't come back. I was called in, sent back, and called back in again. An ultrasound was done, and I was told I was twenty-four weeks along. Six months. I wasn't a candidate for an abortion.

The walls literally came tumbling down. I walked out in tears, sobbing and walked the 4.5 miles home. What was I going to do? How was I going to do it? How was I six months pregnant? The months of denial had caught up to me, and my options were limited. I was terrified and felt utterly alone.

My relationship with my mother had always been a difficult one. It completely ceased after I moved out a few months before. Besides, I thought, she would never be the shoulder I needed right then. Most of my friends were moving on with college and their lives.

How was I supposed to tell him? Doubt rang through my head. He would deny it was his or ask why I had waited so long. Every situation I looked at was filled with shame and fear. I cried the entire walk home, incapable of coming up with an escape plan.

First, I sat my roommate down and told her. She was ecstatic. You'd have thought I was naming her Godmother. She took me to Social Services, where I signed up for food stamps, medical, and welfare.

The welfare system was not interested in the fact that I was going into my seventh month of pregnancy and had no food, or medical assistance, and they certainly were not going to speed things up for me. I was living on one meal a day, mostly peanut butter, sausage, and potatoes. Eventually, aide kicked in, and food was plentiful.

I found a doctor within walking distance who assured a very frightened me that the baby was healthy and growing. With the basic necessities of life at hand, I could finally allow the happiness of this baby to sink in; the kicks, the movements were all measurements of life and health.

Slowly, I started to acquire small items like socks and bibs. Whenever I had a spare dollar here or there, it would go toward the baby. I was finally allowed to revel in this. I was going to have this baby, this baby of sheer denial. It was meant to be and once again, I was in love. In absolute and fully committed love of this child within.

I still hadn't spoken with my mother. We had a very contentious relationship for years. She was controlling and had a drinking problem, and things were made worse when I entered into my teens. Not speaking with her was a mixed blessing because I didn't have to fear her judgment, but I also didn't have the guidance I so desperately needed.

In my eighth month, a wonderful family friend contacted me. He wasn't judgmental. Instead, he offered me two pieces of wisdom: one, an enclosed pamphlet, and the other, the advice to make contact with my mother. The pamphlet was for a local adoption agency, and it sat for a week or more, untouched. But I did contact my mother.

I knew it would be a hard journey to see her. My mother always frightened me, and I was always the child that deep down wanted to please her. This situation was far from pleasing. She cried when she opened the door and there stood her baby with a belly out to here. We talked. She asked me if I understood what I was getting into. She did her standard tough love sell, telling me she would be there for me, but not with a baby. I stood firm with her and told her I was having this baby. For the first time in our relationship, she couldn't just demand me to do something, and have it be done. We had come to this wall, of wanting to be mother and daughter once again, but with new rules.

A few days later I opened the pamphlet. Something in me, to this day I don't know what it was, made me pick up the phone and call them. I wanted to weigh out my options. I explained that I had no intention of giving up my baby, but I was still curious. They sent a worker to see me that week.

The caseworker was a sweet Latina, probably no more than ten years my senior. She never did a hard sell, ever. She just waited for the questions. They came, in small spits. Most were what-ifs and hows. She showed up and took me to lunch once a week like clockwork, still never overselling her position. She soon became my friend and the shoulder I needed to lean on. I still folded and fingered my small trove of baby clothes all the time, imagining the life that laid within me. Was it a little girl who would love ballet, or a little boy who would surf? Would this child ever know their father? I was scared of the unknown.

The drugs at the house were getting worse though, and fear was seeping in at the back of my brain. Did I want to raise my newborn in a house like this? What other options did I have?

One night after a weekend with my mother, I came home back to my decrepit little drug house with my cousin in tow, only to find my room had been ransacked. Things were missing. No one else was home, so my cousin stormed into my roommate's room, and hidden here and there were my things. She packed me up that night and took me back to my mother's.

Coming home, things got real for me, very fast. I knew my options. I could take this precious living being inside of me, and struggle with my limited education, living back in a neighborhood I just came from. But, if I really and truly loved this child with the intensity that I screamed, was offering him or her this life nothing more than a hollow scream? I had to question if I was in love with loveand not with the reality.

Two weeks before my due date, I called the worker and told her I was willing to put the baby up for adoption. As I write these words, more than thirty years later, I have tears in my eyes. My mother was relieved. I vacillated between relief and sadness.

At 11:30 on a rainy January night, my contractions started. I quietly woke my stepdad, who took me to the hospital. I told him he could leave a short time later because I thought I would be fine. I was eighteen and alone. I had no clue. No class, nothing that would tell me what I was in store for. I was just another teen pregnancy to the nurses here.

After an emergency C-section, I woke hours later to a nurse with a heavy Filipino accent telling me I needed to turn over, so I didn't end up with pneumonia. I was groggy and couldn't move, as my abdominal muscles had just been sliced through, and all I could ask was for my baby. "Where is my baby? What sex is it?" She was surprised to know I didn't know, and came back to tell me he was a healthy baby boy. I fell back asleep and woke later to them wheeling this tiny infant into my room.

He was so small, a little over six pounds. I knew nothing about babies. I carefully held him and unwrapped the blanket and counted his toes and fingers. He was absolutely beautiful.

For six days, I held him. I talked to him. I apologized to him and told him how much I loved him. I promised him the perfect family that he would appreciate and deserve. I learned to change his diaper, and I bottle-fed him. I stared at him and he at me. I poured everything I could, every ounce of me into him, hoping for some sort of lasting imprint.

I named him Joshua David. Joshua because I loved the name. David after my brother and grandfather. I knew that his new family would change his name, but I still wanted something of me to say, "Hey, I was here. I loved you. You were my baby Joshua."

My mother surprised me by coming to see the baby. She was kind and a little removed, which was par for the course for my mother. I appreciated what it took for her to do this.

Last was my caseworker, who came by with the final signature, advising the hospital that the agency was permitted to take him home. The day I was discharged, I was a wreck. No one ever wants to leave a hospital without their child. I asked to see him one more time and tears welled up and I silently begged for forgiveness from this tiny week-old infant and said goodbye.

My stepdad took me home. It had been raining for a week. It felt like the earth was weeping along with me, and when I walked in the door, I cried a river of tears I had never ever felt before, until I fell into a deep sleep.

Life started to form back to a regular routine. The adoption worker was still seeing me. The baby was in a temporary home with a woman who did just this, cared for the newborns in between the hospital and their permanent homes. He was doing wonderfully, I was told. Happy and healthy. There were still two hurdles: picking a family and having the birth father relinquish his rights.

I settled for family W, a nice Lutheran family. She had endometriosis and couldn't have children of her own. She had a career in the media and was also a writer, but she would be giving up her job to raise her child. He was a technical director. She was dark like I was, he was tall and fair like the baby's father. They were very well off, and owned a wonderful home in Glendale.

My mother surprised me one weekend and took me shopping. She wanted me to pick out an outfit for him to be taken home from the foster family to his new family. We baby clothes shopped and bonded as she marveled at how much baby clothes had changed since I was little. No more tiny buttons. Everything was snaps and zippers. I finally decided on a creamy yellow sleeper with a hat and blanket. I don't think I ever told my mother how much that meant to me.

I had also kept a journal through the pregnancy. I had written in it fiendishly once I realized I was putting him up for adoption. I wanted him to read and understand it.

February 14th was the last time I saw my worker. She picked me up and took me for Chinese food. I gave her the outfit and the blanket and the journal. She told me the agency would have to go through and white out any identifiable remarks that showed who I or my family was. Any pages removed would be placed in a folder for him to receive when he turned eighteen.

She also explained that she was able to finally track down the biological father. He had evaded many of her previous attempts. When he came in, she explained he had two options: relinquish all rights to the baby and allow the adoption to move forward, or deny paternity all together. She told me he looked at her and said, "He'll know I did this. He'll know I denied him at some point, won't he?" She explained it was a possibility and he said, "He's going to hate me," and then signed that paper.

I called her two days later and told her I had picked a family. She was thrilled. I told her I settled on the W family. What happened next always amazed me. She happily blurted out their last name, exclaiming how thrilled they would be. My mind grabbed that tidbit before anything could change. She got quiet for a moment, and then it was business as usual. She knew. She knew I knew. But I never did anything with it, except hold onto it.

A month after that, a package arrived from the agency. In it was a three-page, beautifully written letter and two photographs. My son was sleepily being held, wearing that beautiful yellow sleeper, wrapped in the blanket. He had fattened up from the hospital. He had the smallest sleepy grin on his face, and his complexion was that perfect apricot hue that only babies have.

The letter writer was the adoptive mother, who went on to tell me how she could never thank me enough for the wonderful gift I had given her and her husband. How hard she knew it had to be on me. She told me of the countless miscarriages she had suffered and the heartbreak it caused her, but she knew it was nothing compared to what I must have gone through.

Then she ended the letter telling me that she would always speak fondly of me to her son, telling him what a precious gift he was given twice, once to be loved so much by someone who wanted a better life for him, and then again by a family who loved him so.

I cherish that letter to this day.

Gina Curvin is the author of a small blog about rediscovering her single self in her middle-aged years. Having moved to South Orange County fifteen years ago with her youngest daughter in tow, she has adjusted to the Stockholm Syndrome of living behind Southern California's infamous Orange Curtain. Since then she has survived raising a teenager, learned she is incapable of raising a dog, and is in the ongoing process of learning how to raise herself.

Bubbe's Story
by Sheila Rosenburg

It has been said that the reason your mother can push all your buttons is because she invented them. In my case, my mother must have a secret engineering degree from MIT. Don't get me wrong, my mom is a good woman. A kind woman. A heart-of-gold type of woman. Not the sharpest brick of cheese in the fridge, and that's probably why those buttons light up.

It's likely a generational thing. She came from an era when women were not properly dressed unless they were wearing a hat, men carried hankies in their pockets, and children's shoes were never scuffed. Growing up, her goal was simply to wear a wedding ring and an apron. And she did. Not only that, but she had her "regular" aprons and her "good" aprons for special occasions, like this satin and tulle number she kept on a hanger in the hall closet. Once, she was in the local newspaper for her celebrated apple cake recipe. In the photo, she is shown mixing the batter wearing pearls, a brooch, and that apron, I kid you not.

Maybe she used to have a wild streak, back in the day. There is a story of how her and her buddies skipped school to see a Frank Sinatra concert where she rushed the stage. After high school, she worked as an executive secretary for the Big Guys who ran a department store in downtown Chicago. She credits her high school diploma and her shorthand skills for landing the job. But the biggest spur-of-the-moment moment in her life was breaking a date with her boyfriend to attend a party at a neighbor's house. There was some guy her neighbors wanted her to meet.

"Oh please, I have a boyfriend. Why do I need this?" she thought.

Her mother said, "Go!" Being the dutiful oldest kid, she went.

While she was at the party she was sitting on the couch, and this guy sitting on the other side kept looking over at her, scoping her out. He was handsome and older than her. Two weeks later, they were engaged. Do you know what would have happened to me, had I tried to pull a stunt like that?

Let me tell you, when my Dad was a young man he was gorgeous. I'm talking George Clooney, Robert Preston gorgeous. Sparkling blue eyes. Thick, wavy, black hair that at that time always seemed to have this little curl hanging down in the middle of his forehead. He had just come back from WWII. Before that, he owned a nightclub. No wonder she fell for him. He was this hunk from Texas, 10 years her.

At the party, they talked. They only made plans to go out, and this guy goes to his friends in the kitchen and tells them to get ready; there's going to be a wedding.

I think they had one or two dates. Two months later they were married, and he brought her down to Texas. From what she told me, it wasn't quite a cakewalk at first. Texas in the late 1940's was not so "enlightened" as was Downtown Chicago. It was a very different life, but they made a life together. A good life. They were happily married for almost 61 years, involved in the community, raised a family, and had a huge network of friends.

Knock on wood, it has been a few years since my mom blew the candles on her 85th birthday, and she hasn't slowed down yet. Recently, I was looking at her keychain and there was one of those little keychain cards from a gym.

"Mom," I said, "what is this doing on here?"

"That's where I work out."

I cannot pull myself from Facebook long enough to do a Richard Simmons DVD in my own den, while she pulls on her sneakers and hops on what she calls "the threadmill" with all the muscle men. Hmmm....maybe she's got the right idea.

Remember earlier when I said heart of gold? This woman makes sure her mailman's kids get a Christmas present.

She read somewhere that birds are not getting enough calcium and that worried her. Mom will take eggshells, broil them for a bit in the oven then sprinkle them over bird seed. I don't cook that well for my children.

I have seen her buy food for homeless people at McDonald's. She approaches them and asks them what they want. One woman looked at her like she was going to cry when my mom set down a plate of pancakes in front of her.

Sometimes you need a Captain Marvel Decoder Ring when talking to her. She has told me of my sister-in-law's trouble sleeping due to her "sleep apathy." After running into a childhood friend of mine at the mall, she called to tell me, "she was so thin...she looked emancipated!"

One of the many things she does to keep busy is volunteer at the hospital. And no simple little Candy Striper for her. No, she monitors the waiting room for the ICU. I would rather have a root canal with no pain meds followed by lunch with my husband's old girlfriends than have to sit and watch that sadness all day. She loves it and loves helping and feeling needed. We almost fell out of our chairs laughing when she told us "a man at the hospital was taken off Life Preservers yesterday."

While having dinner with a girlfriend, this woman was telling Mom she went to lunch that day and the restaurant brought her a whole chicken sandwich when she had only ordered a half sandwich. Mom said, "How could they expect you to eat a whole-chicken sandwich? Why didn't they cut it up?"

You cannot make this stuff up. Like I said before, she can light my buttons. I don't cook, sort of do okay on the cleaning part, and do *not* wake up in the morning so I can make breakfast for my husband. I get up in the morning because I have to go to work. She cannot understand women working, children in daycare and women who "rock the boat" in general. She comes from an era when people wrote letters, returned phone calls, and kept promises. Not bad stuff but, sadly, very rare nowadays. I tell her she expects too much out of people.

Sometimes I'll hang up the phone from a conversation with her, fuming how she doesn't "get it" and I have the urge to send an email to my sister, who has to handle Mom much more than I do since she still lives in our hometown. I type so fast there are sparks flying from my fingers, I'm so angry. My sister taught kindergarten for more than twenty years and knows how to handle her. Nothing seems to faze my sister. Somewhere in a basement someone is making a tiara for my sister for this ability alone.

But you know what? The woman is in her eighties, runs circles around me, makes sure her other elderly friends eat and take their meds. For many years, she had a list of widows that she would call on the phone every night to make sure they were okay.

Heart of gold, that woman.

Sheila Wilk Rosenberg was born and raised in San Antonio, TX. After graduating UT Austin, she married and moved to Dallas. She has two sons. For a few years Sheila also wrote a humor column called "Stretch Remarks." Sheila and her late first husband were involved in two comedy improv troupes. Sheila has since been remarried to a wonderful man. There are now five kids and each has their own "zest."

St. Lucia
by Susan Olson

Early morning, she was awake and chattering. She grabbed the Lucia crown I gave her the night before and put it on her head. It was green with five plastic candles encircling. Double A batteries set them ablaze, with tiny orange flickering points. The crown was just a bit too big for her head. It slipped over one eye, rakishly. She grinned and dug into her Cheerios.

I bought that crown at a Swedish gift shop in California a decade ago in an act of unfettered optimism. It was for the daughter I didn't know that I would ever have. But there she was, all wide smiles and missing teeth and twisting a braid with her fingers as she ate.

I pointed her to a video linked to my Facebook page by a Swedish friend, and she watched it, her face mashed up close to the screen to pick out the face of the 14-year-old chosen to play Lucia on Swedish National Television.

The girl playing Lucia was beautiful, and she walked with such grace that one would think she always walked around with lit candles in her hair. Selam's finger traced her movements on the screen. She was enchanted. She watched the broadcast throughout breakfast and was disappointed to have to shut it off. Selam didn't seem to notice that this particular Lucia's brown skin was at all unusual. She didn't seem to notice the vast sea of blond children singing with the only brown girl playing the leading role. I loved that.

I grew up enchanted by St. Lucia. At the time, the Scandinavian festival represented everything luminescent and extraordinary that I only wished I could manufacture in my workaday Midwestern life. Though I had never seen a live procession, I imagined it all: the white dresses with red sashes, the candles lit in gleaming crowns, voices pure and unison. Every December 13th, I'd jam my feet into dingy snow boots and trudge through mean grey snow, dreaming of white, dreaming of candles, dreaming of the light that would break through the endless grey.

She wanted to wear the crown to school. I hesitated. "Some kids," I said, "might think it's a little weird, you know." I was imagining the older children who sometimes enter the building at the primary grade door in order to deposit younger siblings. She insisted that she didn't care. She *really* wanted to show her teacher, she said.

"Besides," she pointed out, quoting a video we'd watched the night before about Lucia Day, "we light candles to defeat the darkness and the night." Seriously, how could I not let her wear the crown with such an earnest rationale?

She swaggered into the building after enjoying the confused but enthusiastic compliments of parents in the parking lot and burst into her classroom, beaming. I followed her and hovered at the door. Two boys started it. They burst into laughter and pointed at her, forming a tight semi-circle around her. I had heard the term "laugh and point" my whole life but had not seen it in action before. It was ugly. Other children joined in. Maybe a half-dozen kids were participating. In just a few giant steps, I was across the room and at her side. Selam turned her head to me and started to cry; her tears dampened my sweater at the waist. The two instigators followed her and stood close to me. I turned my head and glared and they walked away, still chuckling. It lasted forever.

The teacher was busy talking with another parent about an assignment. I could tell she saw what was going on, but couldn't disentangle herself. I got Selam slowed down and we put her coat and her backpack away. I took the crown and told her that I would bring it back after school, if she wanted, so she could show her teacher.

Selam was still crying quietly. "Don't make me stay," she said.

I was so tempted to take her home.

"Let's go into the hall for a while," I said, but before we could get there the teacher inserted herself and got Selam to talk about the crown. After Selam had recited her piece, including the part about defeating the darkness and the night, Mrs. Porter asked her why she was crying, and Selam told her. The teacher told her that sometimes people just laugh when they are happy, and her candles just made them smile. Selam believed her, or at least pretended to believe her, and agreed to keep the crown at school, hoping to use it for show and tell time.

I spent the day worrying, envisioning all manner of first grade drama. When the phone rang from her school just twenty-five minutes before the final bell, I pounced on it. It was just a robo-call about a band concert. At 2:40, I cautiously rounded the corner to her classroom. Peering into her room, I saw that she was all smiles. She was letting other children try on her crown. When I persuaded her to leave, they groaned.

We went to the library and then to Girl Scouts. The crown went to both places, though she did replace the crown with her Daisy beanie for the meeting.

After the meeting, she put her crown back on. It was still lit. We drove away, her little head glowing in the back seat. It being a holiday and all, I let her talk me into a pancake house for dinner. She wore the crown inside. People stopped and asked her about it. Many thought it had something to do with Hannukah, but she patiently explained over and over again. Every time, she said, "We light candles to defeat the darkness and the night."

Bedtime came quickly and we were reading in her room. She began to cry.

"I really didn't like it when kids laughed at me," she said.

"I know baby. I'm really sorry they did that."

"Mrs. P says it's because they were happy but I don't think all of them were. I think some were happy and others were mean."

"I don't know, baby."

"I just wish they knew that the candles are important. We need them to defeat the darkness and the night. You really shouldn't laugh at that."

"I know, baby."

"And the boys and girls who weren't Lucia, they all had candles too, just not in their hair. Everybody had candles and it was very dark, and then it wasn't. Because there were candles. But Juan and Ian laughed at that. And it's not funny."

I put her to bed, and settled myself into my chair next to her. Suddenly, I remembered the crown, abandoned but still glowing in the front hallway. I retrieved it and set it on her floor.

"I want to hold it again," she whispered, her voice a silver fog halfway to sleep.

I gave it to her, and she drifted away, clutching the plastic crown with its five glowing lights. When I heard her soft and even breaths, I quietly took it from her hands and set it back in the center of her floor, where she would see it again in the morning and remember about the day when the darkness tried but could not overcome. The day when five tiny candles overpowered night.

When I was in the process of adopting Selam, I was sent to so many training programs. I had to learn about multi-racial families and reactive attachment disorder. There were classes on hair care, where I plaited the hair of disembodied doll heads. Her special medical needs resulted in more classes about medications and laws. I took detailed notes on nutrition and milestones. I learned CPR and First Aid and how to outfit my home to survive a fire. Nobody taught me about this, though. Nobody taught me how to outfit her heart to survive first grade. Nobody taught me about the constant tear at your heart, when you let a precious soul out into a world that only sees darkness where her eyes see candles.

A day later, I warily let her back into the first grade room, skirting the gap-toothed villains, willing myself to remember that they are children of God. They were actually children, of course. I kissed her smooth brown forehead and left. "Have the happiest," I said and slipped out the door, willing myself to smile.

Thirty minutes later and just twenty-six miles away, twenty other first-graders were shot by a sole gunman. He entered a pair of classrooms just like hers, where the allegiance had been pledged and the milk mustaches wiped, and gunned them down. I spent the day refreshing the computer screen between every task: sent an email, checked the news, met with a student, checked the news, adjusted a budget, checked the news. It was as if by checking the news, I could find a loophole, a way out. The gunshot sounds were just trucks on a highway, the dead were goldfish. I tried to remember my geography of Newtown, check on friends that lived nearby. The backdrop of all of it, though, was Selam. It was her face I longed to see and my mind's eye was of her in bed the night before, clutching the glowing crown so tightly, hanging on to the departing light.

I snuck out of work early; I had to pick her up from after-care. I *had* to see her. When I got to the center, she was in the pool. I watched from the observation window; a silent movie of six-year-olds at play. Tears welled, but I swallowed them in time to wrap her in a thick towel, and lost myself in the mundane act of dressing a wet child.

"Here," I said, handing her a sweater I had just untangled. "It's cold out." She fought me on it. "Just wear it," I whined. "Wear it because you can," I thought, then chastised myself for caring about sweaters at all. She put it on, and pouted.

Two days later, *Gaudete* Sunday, we prepare to head to church. We had been invited to light the third advent candle at the church we attend. We had practiced for days, and Selam could not have been more proud to show the congregation her developing reading skills. That morning, she announced at breakfast, "Really, lighting the candles is very, very important, Mommy, much more important than anything else."

I had to agree. She recited her lines over and over again from the back seat, as the car twirled through crooked roads. Clad in red and white, we took the stone stairs into the stone New England church. Her curls caught the light as she ascended before me. She stopped to invite a classmate to admire her new shiny shoes, not yet scuffed. Her broad smile delighted me. Once inside, though, she stopped short.

The congregation was subdued. The evergreens wilted in the face of the congregation's stiff sorrow. Selam had been told about Sandy Hook in the broadest, most general strokes. I suspect that by Sunday, she had forgotten it. She slowed her steps and we walked to the front to be seated, her face a puzzle. The whole thing was wrong. The pink candle seemed out of place, and the call to worship must have been written for another community, another world where schools were safe and the Third Sunday in Advent was the call to rejoice. Around me, faces were tightly drawn. Next to me was Selam, swinging her legs, admiring her shoes, practicing her words under her breath. I squeezed her close, thinking of twenty-six miles difference, thinking of the candles, of the words, and the new shoes. It all mixed together.

The organ played. We sang. We prayed. We choked out the call to worship, and listened to the thin announcements. Everyone was waiting for the children to leave, I could tell.

It was time, then, and my daughter and I walked to the chancel. I took the candle lighter, and lit the purple candles: one, two. Selam read, "We have lit the candles of Hope and Peace." She paused and looked up at me. I nodded encouragement. "Now, we light the candle of JOY!" She bellowed the last word, bouncing up on her toes, and escaping into a broad grin. Her voice echoed in the white-washed room, and she stood on tip-toe, her face awash with expectation. The congregation hesitated a second, and then smiled and a few chuckles rang forth.

I looked at her, and the candles, and the people ahead of us. I had no answers, really, to any of it. I couldn't stop children from laughing at what was different. I couldn't stop confused young men from careening through the hearts of children and families just like mine. There was good and there was evil and it was all right there in my arm's reach. There was a line to walk, like those balance beam exercises back in high school gym class, where we'd step three times, then dip one foot down below the slender beam. I could do it, so long as I kept my eyes forward. One glance side-wards, though, and I'd crumple to the mats below.

We finished our liturgy, and Selam hugged me in triumph, and began to head off to Sunday School, full of joy, full of light. I was barely seated when she was back at my side.

"Mommy," she whispered, breathless, "I know why we light candles today." I looked up at the three flames dancing on the wreath in front. "We light candles to defeat the darkness and the night."

I didn't know what those words meant to her, this mantra she adopted. But I nodded and hugged her tight.

Perhaps a candle is our best defense against the nighttime that beckons, that dips just below the slender beam. Perhaps it begins with a candle, with the slender pull, the flicker, the scandalous and joyous light.

Susan Olson is a Presbyterian pastor, currently serving as assistant dean of students at Yale Divinity School. She is a graduate of the University of Illinois, Michigan State University, and Yale Divinity School. Ms. Olson is the mother of a brilliant, brave, and beautiful eight-year-old daughter. They make their home in New Haven, CT.

Mom Genes

by Jackie Hennessey

When you turn 40-something, before hyperventilating from the realization that you are actually 40-something, an age that was considered "ancient" when you were a kid, you begin to discover certain things about yourself. Things that you don't necessarily want to post on Facebook.

Like the fact that unless you are a retired runway model, you can no longer get away with wearing a mini skirt. That is, unless you plan on scaring away small children. I know this for a fact because I frightened my own just the other day. I was sitting on the couch in a very short skirt. My legs were crossed. It was a hot-as-jalapenos summer day and because my body was beginning to think it was trapped in a week-long hot flash, I decided to put on a short denim skirt I hadn't worn in years.

Big mistake.

"O M goodness, Mom, what is that," my 10-year-old daughter asked.

"What's what, honey," I said, thinking I had something on my face.

"That," she said, pointing to my thighs, or more accurately, the excess bubbles of flab that had rolled beyond my leg and my skirt and was now suctioned to the leather cushion.

"That," I asked. "Oh, that."

"Yes, are you ok? What *is* that?"

"It's just cellulite."

"Cellulite?"

"Yes, cellulite."

"What is cellulite?"

"It's extra skin, honey. Like on chicken."

"Chicken skin? You have chicken skin on your leg?"

"No," I said out loud, and muttered to myself, "More like chicken fat."

"Oh." Her face was crinkling up like she had swallowed a giant sour gummy worm.

"Yeah, it's like extra chicken skin that just so happens to plop out when you wear an inappropriately short skirt like mommy's."

"Oh," she said, with the same citric expression.

How else do you explain flab to a 10-year-old without scarring her for life before she even reaches puberty? I could sense an emotion that fell somewhere between shock and sympathy on her face, but the air fell silent. And awkward. But no one had passed gas. I knew in my heart that it would be best for everyone if I just shut my mouth and went upstairs to fetch a pair of pants. Thankfully, we never spoke of it again.

I realized that in a few short years, going shopping with mom is going to be more "torture" than a "treat" for my daughter, even if it includes an entourage of friends and a stop at the local frozen yogurt shop. So I celebrated her still liking me, and we drove to the mall with big smiles on our faces.

We had a ball, walking around the adorable shops, trying on sunglasses and scarves, smelling candles and gathering home design and fashion ideas.

Then suddenly, like a sugar crash following a fro-yo with extra sprinkles, my mood changed. The moment we walked into a store that was one of my favorites in my 20's and 30's, the ugly truth came to me.

The mannequins looked anemic. Every skirt was too short. Every top was way too trendy. And every pair of skinny jeans looked like they were made for an doll. Whether I wanted to believe it or not, I had outgrown this store, and it had outgrown me too. You know you've outgrown your favorite clothing store when everything seems way too trendy, the sales associates don't even bother to make eye contact with you, you try on one pair of "stretchy skinny jeans" and get depressed, nothing fits no matter what you try on, the horrid lights in the fitting room accentuate every lump you didn't even know you had, and even the headbands are too tight for your head.

As I embrace mid-life with open and flabby arms, I realized something else about myself that I can never take back. This goes beyond boycotting mini-skirts or avoiding my grandmother's favorite clothing store, Chico's, a little while longer for fear that I will be zapped up by the Cocoon ship.

I'm talking about mom genes. No matter how hard I try to avoid it, I have come to the realization that I am slowly turning into my mother. Now, my mother is a sweetheart. She has the biggest heart, and I love her dearly.

But like any mom, she has habits that leave me puzzled, perplexed, and searching for the nearest bag of semi-sweet chocolate chips. Habits like forgetting why she came into a room, carrying on a conversation five rooms away, wearing two pairs of sunglasses at the same time, falling asleep on the couch at 7:30 p.m. and wondering why she can't sleep through the night, using hand gestures while talking on the phone as if the person on the other line can see, or hearing a favorite song on the radio and singing and dancing (oh yes, always dancing) along to it.

My mom single-handedly ruined Van Halen's "Jump" for me because she would "rock out" to it every time the song came on the radio. And her version of "rocking out" was flailing her arms back and forth like we did when we took Jazzercise class together in the 1980's. To this day, I hear the song and automatically experience a Pavlovian hankering to pull on a pair of leg warmers and "skip, ball, change" to the oldies.

My mom and I, to my husband's dismay, seem to share a laundry basket of Mom Genes. In fact, I'm wearing two pairs of glasses as I write this. And I woke up from my couch "nap" at 9 p.m.

But nothing measures up to the day I heard myself ask my daughter from outside a dressing room, "Does the crotch fit?" At that moment, I knew I was a goner. As the words escaped my mouth, I flashed back to 1984, inside a cramped, neon-pink dressing room at Express.

"Honey, does the crotch fit?"

"Oh whatever, mom, please stop," I pleaded, trying on a pair of Express jeans, straight from the sales rack.

"You have to make sure the crotch fits," she said, loud enough for the Orange Julius vendor to hear.

"Ok, I know, mom. But, like, please stop."

"They won't last a week if the crotch doesn't fit right."

When I walked out, I noticed the crotch was a little tight. "Dang it," I thought, "like, she was totally right."

I also noticed that one of the most popular girls in my school was standing right there. The whole time. Her jaw dropped as low as "Heathers," along with my already tween-sized self-esteem.

Ah, motherhood. Because, as moms, we have it coming to us. My kids tend to get annoyed by me, too. It's already starting. They are great kids, but they can't help themselves. I have started to annoy my 13-year-old son to such a degree that I think just being in his presence when we're in public is an embarrassment. When I hear a familiar song on the radio, I can't help myself and start rocking out. I actually do this whether in the car, kitchen, or other "OMG" public places.

"Mom, stop," my son pleads.

"Use your manners."

"Mom, please stop," he says.

"I can't. I like the beat."

"I love you, but, I'm walking away now."

Next thing I know, my 10-year-old daughter is in the room. As soon as she absorbs the scene from the Prince song playing to me cackling out loud, she does the only sensible thing any mortified 10-year-old can do. She closes her eyes.

"My eyes are burning, Mom. Please stop."

I pretend to not hear her. It's the artist otherwise known as Prince back when he was Prince, so I have to keep going.

"Ain't no particular sign I'm more compatible with," I sing, totally out of tune.

"Mom, please stop!"

"I just want your extra time and your…." And my hips are rolling like a mother.

I keep dancing, busting out and moving to the music, and I'm realizing I'm looking more and more like my favorite Smother from the Goldbergs, to my utter dismay. And, oh yes, my daughter's eyes are still closed. Then she leaves the room. Finally, the song ends, along with my dance. Pay back may be a biiaaatch, but sometimes you have to dance it out.

Something else I've realized about myself that I've inherited from my mother is that I am pale. I mean, really pale. Everyone around me has skin pigmentation at least two Crayola shades darker than mine. If you're peach, I'm egg shell. Apricot? I'm chalk. Burnt sienna? I'm not even in the carton. Let me put it this way: If I stood in front of a cream-colored wall in a cream-colored outfit, you would see nothing but my hair and eyes. I mean it. Nothing else. Just hair and eyes. My dad is naturally tan, but my mom is extremely fair. Thanks for the white legs, mom! Thanks again for the mom genes!

I have a feeling that my children, who have suffered since birth from my over-SPF-with-long-sleeve-swim-T's mothering protection, will be venting about my pale mom genes in their forties. Who am I kidding? They've secretly been cursing me from underneath the beach umbrella since they were toddlers. Thankfully, I have come a long way from 1980-something days of water skiing with tan accelerator slathered all over my body or laying out at the beach without using an ounce of sunscreen.

Recently, when my husband and I were out at the movies with our kids, I laughed out loud so loudly in the middle of a funny scene, no one could hear what the actress said next. I couldn't help it – it was really funny. So I laughed out loud. Or, as kids these days say, LMAO (an acronym I finally "got" a few years ago). After the movie, as we're walking to the car, my son pats me on the head, gives me a hug and says, "That's my mom."

So, that's my legacy. In twenty years, my children will forget all the things I did for them. The hugs, the packed lunches, the homemade cookies, unearthing answers to questions, the endless errands, the free round-trip mom-taxi service. All of it will be zapped from their memories. But the cackling so loudly that no one in the entire movie theater can hear the next line…that's what they will remember about their mother.

Since reaching my forties, I've discovered a lot of things about myself. And in the process, I've realized how important it is to not be afraid to be myself. And to embrace my laughing out loud. My rolls. My pale legs. My belly laughing. My friendliness. My dancing. My gabbiness. All of my mom genes. Even the pair of sunglasses that have been sitting on top of my head since this morning.

Jackie Hennessey moved from Texas to Rhode Island in high school and lives there now with her husband and two children. She has worked full-time, part-time, and been a stay-at-home mom. Jackie blogs about her take on motherhood at <u>Ventingsessions.com</u>, writes about it in her award-winning book, <u>How to Spread Sanity on a Cracker</u>, and has vented about it in front of live audiences, including the Providence Listen to Your Mother show. This former journalist-turned-public-relations-consultant is a graduate of Texas A&M University, where she received the "Best Aggie-Life writer" award.

Enough

by Nanci Rathbun

The ideal mom? Margaret Anderson from *Father
Knows Best* comes to mind. She knew best, too, and often
got husband Jim out of a tight spot. Or Donna Stone from
The Donna Reed Show. Kind, but firm, she kept her
children from going down the wrong path. Maybe Ma from
Little House on the Prairie, with her deep faith and
hardworking determination. While these women faltered
occasionally, they were rooted in strong values that
centered on their families. As a child, I read about them or
watched them and wondered, why is my family so
different? Why doesn't my mom act like that?

I longed for a mother like those fictional moms and
was painfully aware that my family was not ideal. I felt
shame about it. My dad was a drinker – we didn't use the
word 'alcoholic' back then – and my mom worked hard to
hold the family together. 'Enabler' was a term that I
learned much later in my life.

Dad was a quiet drunk, a beeraholic, who generally
ignored us kids. Words from Dad were few and far
between. They held a lot of weight. My sister Barb was
athletic and so earned his occasional praise. I was shy and
bookish. He had almost nothing to say to me.

My mother was a stay-at-home mom. My father
made a career in the Army. To conceal the drinking
problem, my parents frequented a local tavern off-base.
Barb and I spent many nights doing homework at a booth,

while my parents occupied stools at the bar. Mom would order food and make sure we had what we needed to get our work done, while supervising my dad. Since she never learned to drive, she focused on keeping him sober enough to get us home safely. Many nights, Barb and I sat in the back seat while Mom called, "Bob, be careful, the kids are in the car!" in a subdued shout at my dad.

So ours was not a *Father Knows Best* family. Most of the credit for my sister's and my own relative sanity goes to our mom.

She did the usual mom things. Every morning, until we were teenagers, she got up, made coffee in a percolator, and cooked breakfast. She made sure our school clothes were clean and pressed, and that was no small chore before the days of electric washers and dryers. She used a wringer washer and hung the clothes on a clothesline outside in warm weather or draped them over a wooden clothes rack in the winter. There wasn't any permanent press until the sixties, so everything was ironed. That took her an entire day, since Dad's khakis had to be specially starched, rolled, and stored in the refrigerator until ready to be pressed.

When we got home after school, there was usually a snack and milk. Mom didn't believe in Kool-Aid, and we were jealous of our friends who got to drink it. We had to change into play clothes first because money was tight and we couldn't spill on our school clothes or damage them. When we were stationed overseas, Mom ordered from the Spiegel catalog twice a year, using funds provided by her father back in the States. Whatever we got had to last until the next order. Barb and I would tell Mom about school and homework assignments and maybe get a chance to play outside.

When Dad got home from his Army accountant's job, he changed out of uniform and opened the first beer of the day. Sometimes we had supper at home. Mom was a good cook and tried to cater to Dad's tastes and stay within a slim food budget. Buying beer and cigarettes was the first priority. Quite often, we headed for the tavern and supper was a sandwich or a bar pizza.

Mom made sure that drinking didn't start before the end of the work day, that Dad got food as well as beer into his stomach, and that he was in bed in enough time to be functional the next morning. My sister and I were expected to "be good," which meant that we were to be quiet, respectful, and diligent about our schoolwork. We knew that once Dad was home, attending to him came first for Mom. We also knew that should we get into trouble at school or in the base housing, it would rebound onto Dad. Heaven forbid that he should be disciplined because of us. It would mean a cut in pay: a disaster the family could not absorb.

Barb and I played with the other Army brats. Being on base housing gave us a lot of freedom. We played kickball on the playground and there were lots of places to engage in hide-and-seek or build a fort with blankets and spend summer days inside the shelter with our friends and our dolls or books, emerging for lunch and then disappearing until supper. We went to good schools, both on base and off. Mom sent us to catechism classes and Dad delivered us to the base church for Mass, although they never went to church themselves. With Mom raised a Roman Catholic and Dad a Lutheran, there was a lot of family dissension about their marriage. Their solution seemed to be to ignore religion themselves.

Mom read to us and bought books with funds she squirreled away from the milk money or bakery money. I don't think I'd be a writer today if not for my mother's attention to reading. She played games with us and I particularly remember how fun it was to be sick, because I could stay home from school and have Mom's undivided attention. She always let me win at Monopoly. She fixed cups of sweet hot tea and urged me to drink them. She toasted bread, buttered it, and spread jam on it. I thought it was heavenly because I knew in those precious hours that she really, truly loved me.

Our relationship degenerated when I reached my teen years and my father's drinking worsened. By then, he was retired from the Army. I was ashamed to bring friends home. I resented that there was money for beer and cigarettes, but none for music lessons or clothes. I took my first job at age fifteen, and from then on, I paid my own way and even earned enough to cover the tuition costs at the Catholic high school I was enrolled in. I dismissed my mother as weak, as complicit in my father's drinking, as uncaring about my sister and me.

When I married young and became a mother myself, I longed for the kind of support from my parents that my peers had: presents for my daughter, offers to babysit, motherly advice, fatherly play with the kids. But Mom was so busy supporting my father, whose alcoholism had damaged his liver and eyesight, that she could do little more than admire her first grandchild on an occasional visit.

It wasn't until my father died in his early sixties that I reclaimed a sense of closeness with Mom. I was a single parent by then, having divorced when my son was only two, working long hours to support my little family. I could call Mom and vent – about work, about bills, about the frustrations of parenting. She listened, not judging me. She liked to go shopping with me when I needed new business clothes. I think she took a vicarious pleasure in my career. She loved her grandkids, my two and my sister's two, and liked lavishing small gifts on them and going to their school events. Maybe it gave her a sense of fulfillment for the times she couldn't do those things for Barb or me.

Then the illnesses came. Breast cancer, atrial fibrillation, COPD, cancer of the mouth. Barb and I became Mom's parents, while trying to parent our own kids and work and keep our households running. I was angry that Mom's years of smoking and drinking—although I don't recall ever seeing my mother drunk, she drank to keep Dad company and manage him—likely contributed to those health issues. I didn't want to be her mother. I wanted *her* to be *mine*.

When cancer recurred in her knee and cancer of the mouth made it impossible for her to take solid food, she gave up her little apartment and moved into my condo. By then, my kids were grown and on their own. I was starting to devote serious time and effort to my writing and was in the midst of a course in lay ministry through my denomination. I had to scale down on those things, things that gave me joy and meaning. Mom was sick and she came first, rather like my dad came first all those years ago.

I came to understand that, all along, Mom did the best she could. It wasn't perfect. She was never Mrs. Cleaver, but she gave all that she had, as limited as it might have been. I wanted that *Leave It to Beaver* family when I was a girl. I longed for steadfast fatherly love and guidance, for sweet motherly attention and sharing, but what I got was enough. Enough to mold me into a strong woman who could raise her kids on her own. Enough to teach me the values of hard work and perseverance, of the miracle of undivided attention. Enough to ground me in faith, even though I left that early faith tradition. Enough to give me a lifelong love of learning and the written word. Enough.

When all is said and done, enough is all we have. I've made my own mistakes as a child and a wife and a parent, but I always tried to do the best I could. I think my mom did, too.

Perhaps the best we can hope for is that we get enough to grow into our own role in life. Thanks, Mom. You did enough. I love you for that.

Nanci Rathbun is a longtime Wisconsin resident who is planning an upcoming move to the West Coast to be closer to her grandchildren – oh, and their parents. Her first novel, <u>Truth Kills: An Angelina Bonaparte Mystery</u>, was published in 2013. <u>Cash Kills</u> is the second book in the series and was published in November of 2014. The first chapters of each on her web site or on Goodreads. The third Angie novel has a working title of <u>Deception Kills</u>, with plans to publish in 2015.

Touch

by Sharon Laidlaw-Almaguer

"Fifteen minutes," my mother answered, keeping her eyes trained on her hands, which were neatly folding sandwiches into waxed paper on the counter.

Fifteen minutes. That was how long you had to leave it in for.

I was 13, desperate for information about what was coming next, and all I'd gotten from my mom was a thin book with a staid gray cover: *A Doctor Talks to 9-12 Year Olds*. "Let me know if you have any questions," she'd told me, as she began her evening routine of packing lunches, but with greater focus than ever before.

I had run to my room and devoured the booklet, flipping quickly past the pages of diagrams of child bodies transforming into adult bodies, scanning for the information I hadn't already gotten in school. And I had found it. Somewhat. There, under a drawing of a man and a woman lying next to each other in bed, discretely covered by a sheet, was a single paragraph which began, "When a man loves a woman very much, they lie together, his penis becomes hard, and…"

My mom had given me an opening to ask questions, and I doubted the opportunity would present itself again. I was determined to make the most of it. But the only question I could think to form out of the chaos that single paragraph had left in my brain was, "How long do you have to leave it in for?"

Fifteen minutes.

It's likely that's what she had learned in her years of marriage to my father—fifteen minutes on a really good day, I'm guessing. They were married for 32 years, but I rarely saw anything pass between them that resembled intimacy. I vaguely recall him asking my mother for a peck on the lips while she cooked, maybe. He died in that thirty-second year of marriage after a long illness, during which she had nursed him, day after day and night after night. In the week immediately following my father's death, I helped her clear out his things; she was a practical person at the core, and it was impractical to keep his clothes and papers lying around when he was no longer there to use them. While we dug through my father's things, she opened up a bit about their marriage in all its bittersweet complexity. In this new conversational territory for us, she spoke quietly, pronouncing each word with a careful deliberateness. Her phrasing was like fishing line, tossed tentatively in different directions until she found something she could manage. The idiom she finally reeled in was: "to have relations."

This marked the second—and last—time in my life that I talked with my mother about sex.

Years later, while my mother was dying from cancer and her body was wasting away, I spent a lot of time touching her. She needed help with the basics, first of all. Also, she dropped sizes so quickly that we spent a fair amount of time in mall dressing rooms, adjusting straps and sliding zippers over thin skin. When she lay in bed resting, I'd brush her hair, scratch her back, massage her feet, and wonder when her body had last felt loving touch from a human being other than her three children. I wondered if the starvation her body must have once felt for touch was so long repressed that it didn't even register anymore. Regardless, I made my touch warm and loving and confident against her weak, chemical-infused form, to give evidence to my words, to let her know that she was loved and safe.

Physical intimacy is a way of knowing ourselves and others. Yes, it brings us pleasure. But more importantly, it makes us stronger and more complete human beings. Whether it's holding hands, a back rub, or a sexual encounter, we open up ourselves to someone else, and in that experience we learn to trust and be trusted. We learn that no matter how we feel, we are not alone.

I remember when my mother's body provided me with every comfort I knew. I remember climbing onto her lap and resting my head on her chest, on the flat triangle bordered by her collarbone, sternum, and pillowy, pendulous breasts. I would squish back the soft fullness of her belly from where it folded onto her legs. I remember sitting in church, bored out of my skull, tracing the veins on the back of her hand with one little finger, or picking at her cuticles. I remember when, as a teenager, I tried to teach her how to do her makeup, the way her flaccid eyelid skin responded so differently than mine did to the pull of an eyeliner pencil. And reaching back farther than my memory can, there were experiences of breastfeeding, of being bathed by her, of being held and carried. Hers was the first body I knew deeply, the first physical intimacy I had. For a woman who had lived most of her life without enjoying the loving touch of anyone other than her own children, she conveyed her deep, boundless love for us through every cell of her body.

I don't know if she had any memories at all of early physical intimacy; my grandmother died suddenly when my mom was only eight. One day the family found out she had colon cancer. Three days later, she was dead, leaving a gruff, millworker husband, and two daughters: thirteen year-old, girly Claire, and my mom, Jeannette, as rough and tumble as a girl could be in 1951, in that blue-collar, French Catholic town in New Hampshire. She grew up without a mother's warmth. The most influential adult woman in her young life was her Aunt Marguerite, who lived next door and came over every Saturday afternoon to stroke a white-gloved hand on the surfaces of the house, checking Jeannette's and Claire's weekly chores. So it's possible my mother never felt intimacy again after that day that her mother was suddenly taken from her.

Regardless, the photos of my mom from that time show a happy, confident girl with short hair and overalls, legs placed firmly on the ground, hands set on her hips, a wide smile on her face. She was a tomboy. There are pictures of her with her bike leaning up against the front porch, and pictures of her holding a football for her cousins to kick. At around that time, more than anything in the world, my mom wanted a set of toy guns, so she would be properly equipped for games of Cowboys and Indians with the neighborhood boys. She begged and pleaded for those guns. She knew she'd look fantastically tough sporting those guns tucked into her waistband, as she rode her trusty Schwinn steed up and down Leonard Street and across vacant lots. She was confident in her physical form and in what her body could do when she went out to play with the boys. Her dad gave her a doll, instead, as a joke. She hurled it at him, before he revealed the coveted guns. Forget dolls and their associated frills or heels or skirts or hairpins; those guns were just the accessories she needed. I heard this story many times growing up, and the sparkle in her eye and lack of remorse when she told it showed that the tough little girl was still very much alive in the grown woman.

When she was too old to use her body for playing outside, she used it as a means to practical ends. She approached life with the slightly cold reserve that was the cultural norm in small-town New England, so when she finished high school, she went to nursing school, because that seemed like the only option for a young woman who wasn't already engaged. And when she finished nursing school, she went into the convent. The way she put it to me years later, she had three choices: become a hippie, join the war, or become a nun. Having spent twelve years in Catholic school, she chose the devil she knew.

As a geriatric nurse, my mom—"Sister Brian"— learned to care for other people's bodies. I imagine her thin, un-made-up lips pursed professionally as she cleaned bodily fluids, changed sheets, comforted. I imagine her strong, capable, brave hands cupped under an arm, helping a fragile resident rise from a chair. I can see the muscles of her fingers tightening into a fist around a sponge, squeezing soapy water into a bucket before gently wiping the sponge along a curved, age-spotted back.

One of the secrets that died with my mother is whether or not she had any boyfriends before she later married my father at the age of 29. With all the touching she did as a nurse, had she ever touched or been touched in anything other than a clinical way? From all I know of her, I strongly suspect that she had not, that on the fast track through Catholic school, nursing school, and the convent, she perhaps didn't have a kiss from a boy until she met my dad. There were little hints, like when she told me at 16 that I didn't need to see a gynecologist until I was married. Or when, as a preteen, I found initials carved into a desk that had been hers: RH. "Roy Hebert," she told me, with a dreamy look in her eye: a boy she had a crush on in high school. But she never dated him, she added; "He was a popular boy." He never even knew how she felt.

Most people, upon hearing that my mom was a nun before she married and produced a family of three children in three years, assume it was some kind of scandal that pulled her into secular life. But they're wrong. Her departure from the convent was a turning away from scandal, not toward it. "The nuns drank at lunch," my mom would say, when pressed. She spoke about it only in the vaguest of terms: "I couldn't stand the way they acted with each other, the nuns and priests. It wasn't right. There was a lot going on those days that was only talked about in whispers." When she left the convent, armed with her nursing certificate and an affinity for Jack Daniels on the rocks, she was able to make her own way. Just three months after my mom hung up her nun's habit for the last time, a friend introduced her to my father, and they were married within the year.

I distinctly remember the afternoon I did the math and it occurred to me that my birth date, March 20, was six days shy of nine months from the day my parents got married. I was in my bedroom, drifting through random, preteen musings—probably staring up at a poster of Duran Duran—when it hit me. I remember springing down the stairs and cornering my mom. "When you were pregnant with me, what was the date I was due?" I asked. Part of me was excited to catch her with some hard evidence of impropriety. But mostly I had high hopes when I presented her with this information, and I offered it to her less like a gauntlet than like an outstretched hand, offered it in an attempt at connection. But she dodged it. She was quick to tell me the exact date marking nine months from their wedding, and she looked away so abruptly that I wasn't convinced. As an adult, knowing what I know now about the complications of calculating due dates and the slim chance she'd remember an actual, hard-and-fast date twelve years and two babies later, the stating of "March 26th" after a wedding date of "June 26th" seems contrived. What complex conversation might she have been avoiding, I wonder? What might I have learned about my mom's experience of touch if I had been able to explore that answer further?

I knew that her three babies had come fast—both in the short-term context of labors and in the longer context of her marriage—one after the other in those first three years, so that my brothers' infancies were a blur to her later on. She told me about her labors with confidence, the same self-assurance with which she related the stories of a little girl sporting pistols on her hips. As she talked of her now-legendary, lightning-quick, easy deliveries, she held her head up, smiled, and her eyes sparkled. I, the first, had tumbled out in only three hours, and the time was cut in half with each baby afterward until the third sent her rushing to the hospital at the very first contraction.

Caring for newborns was not as seamless, apparently, as pushing them out. I was only 14 months old when her second child was born, and he was only two months old when she learned she was pregnant with a third baby. She went crying to the Monsignor. "What can I do?" she implored. "I can't do this anymore. I just can't."

She couldn't have been the first hysterical, obedient Catholic newlywed to ask this question, and Monsignor was ready with his response: "Use birth control." And she did, she must have, because there the babies ended.

I have told this story so often in my life, explaining the proximity in age of us three siblings and the lack of any more, that I sometimes wonder if I've made it up. Is it possible that a woman could actually get dispensation to stop having babies from an official of the Catholic Church?

Whatever happened in the Monsignor's office that day, she certainly felt excused from ever having to talk about the subject again in the future. She was present for my brothers and me in so many ways. She cuddled and caressed and cleaned and soothed and rocked and sang. She played with us, chauffeured us, encouraged us, and attended every concert, sporting event, and competition. As a child, I prayed passionate prayers that she would live a long time, that she would stay with me forever, because I felt that her love was deep and solid, and the other aspects of my life were not easy. I trusted her. But we did not, ever, talk about how babies were made. For my entire life—with the exceptions of the "fifteen minutes" conversation and the distracted musings as we packed my father's things— she deftly deflected even the slightest hint of the topic.

For this reason—and because I knew my father, who was neither joyful nor sexy—the book title *The Joy of Sex* seemed profoundly ironic when I discovered it one day sitting among the two short, neat rows of books on my mom's dresser. Those dozen or so volumes were the only books my mom owned. There was probably a Bible in there, too, and certainly several cheap mystery paperbacks. *The Joy of Sex* was a flamboyant, irreverent interloper in this otherwise simple, modest display. I spotted it one day when I was sprawled on her bed, chatting with her while she folded laundry. I sputtered and quickly fastened my gaze on the neat piles of shirts, so she didn't notice my distraction. But the next day, when I arrived from school with a few hours to spare before she came home from work, I closed her bedroom door and pulled the book gently from its resting place. The book jacket was folded in at the section titled, *Masturbation.*

From my perspective, holding no small amount of distaste for my dad, the fact that particular chapter was marked needed no explanation.

But *where* and *why* and *how* did my mother acquire that book? Of all the answers that died with my mother, the answers to those questions are high up on the list of those I would like to have heard. Did my father buy it, to try to break through her reserve? Or had she bought that book to try to bring some spark back into their long marriage? Back in the days before Amazon.com, how would a woman like my mother even know such a book existed? Could she possibly have had a friend with whom she was so close that she could discuss "relations" or the lack thereof?

The Joy of Relations.

I believe my mom would have been mystified by the idea of the "joy of sex." Joy equals pleasure, and she was raised in a culture that thought the only kind of pleasure was a guilty one. Like I said, she was a practical woman to the core, and she felt a deep sense of obligation to practicality and the crossed-out to-do lists that are practicality's measures of success. It follows that physical pleasure—being both not practical and inherently devalued because it is "of the flesh"—was something that only the most base people would care about. I don't know if my mom intended to communicate this to me through her body language, example, and her silence about the topic, but she did. Over and over, from her and in Catholic school, I came to understand that the pursuits of the intellect were worthy and good, and pursuits of the body were frivolous, at best. The work of the devil, at worst.

This was not, however, the message I heard in the subtext of whispered conversations at school, or in the lyrics of songs, or in the videos on MTV.

I was left to myself to reconcile those messages. I loved my mom, so she couldn't be *completely* wrong, could she? One of my biggest challenges as an adolescent—hell, for my entire life after the age of fourteen—was to create a paradigm in which my mom's avoidance of the topic of sex could be reconciled with what I saw in the world around me. In what kind of a reality could my mom's delicacy regarding my body exist with her ability to bathe strangers? How could physical intimacy be a topic so awe-inspiring that it drove her to silence, at the same time that it engendered bold communication in song, dance, art, and literature?

In constructing that new paradigm, I read between the lines of the transcripts of my conversations with my mom, remembering the sparkle in her eyes as she recounted the power of her body to easily birth a child, and letting the averted gaze as she stated "fifteen minutes" devolve into the stuff of farce. I hold tightly to my memories of her sighs as I brushed her hair, or to the dreamy look on her face when she told me that, yes, breastfeeding us was wonderful. I remember her strength when she hit a softball harder than any of the other parents at the family picnic, or her grace when she and I water-skied together, and I marvel in my own body's ability to adapt to increasingly challenging exercise routines as I get older.

I choose the lessons I learn by choosing which models I follow, but it's taken years of talking about intimacy with friends and opening myself up to lovers and strangers to undo the education of my mom's silence. I've been deliberate about teaching myself that touching and being touched is both something sacred, and a pleasure I can allow myself to enjoy. Even now, I'm tempted to compare it to something like eating ice cream or buying a new pair of shoes; I fight against this ingrained sense that physical intimacy might be enjoyed, but in moderation only, and that it most correctly comes along with a dose of restraint and a twinge of guilt.

But the legacy ends here. I have my own kids now, and I teach my little guys to love their bodies. I want them to be aware of how much their bodies can do for them, so I comment on the length and strength of their limbs, on the muscular ripples that are forming on their prepubescent frames. I point out my own sense of accomplishment when I exercise and feel strong, balanced, and powerful. I touch them affectionately, and teach them how to touch me affectionately. I help them learn words for gently telling me when my well-intentioned touch doesn't actually feel good to them. I encourage them to be direct when they tell me they want their backs rubbed, to be articulate about where they want it, whether they want light touch or firm pressure, whether they want smooth strokes or scratching. I teach them how to say "no" to each other when their play gets physical, to only say it when they really mean it, and to listen to each other without exception when it's said.

I was one of the first parents among their friends to have "The Talk" with them, when they were eight. It was just the first of many "talks," which are definitely lowercase. I try to talk about physical intimacy with the right mixture of reverence and joy, to somehow normalize it in conversation while helping them understand that it is powerful, special, and often poorly approached. Periodically, when we're driving somewhere and it occurs to me, I'll turn off the radio and ask them if they have any questions about sex. "Anything come up lately that you're curious about or would like to discuss?" And usually the answer is no. But every once in a while they want to verify something overheard at school or in the news or in a song lyric: "Mommy, when that song says, 'Like a virgin, you're Madonna,' what does that mean?" And I give them an answer that does not dodge the complexities of it, that's realistic, and that walks the fine line between sugar-coating or romanticizing intimacy, and scaring them away from it.

When it comes down to it, I want my boys to know from the beginning that—like most things about physical intimacy—"how long you have to leave it in for" is a complex and nuanced concept, indeed: you don't have to leave it in at all; or, you actually do; you want to; you might not want to; you might want to cover it; you might put it in different places; you might want to leave it in longer sometimes than others; "it" can be many different things. And on, and on. These are concepts that I'm sure my mom knew. She just couldn't—absolutely couldn't—verbalize them, maybe not even to herself. A long, rocky, complicated relationship with her body and the bodies of those around her left cloudy layers of doubt on the answers to all of those questions and on her confidence in her own ability to wrap her head around them.

The truth, in all its complicated, emotionally-laden messiness, is my rudder. I follow the truth—*what is it, really?*—in order to pronounce words that still sound awkward and foreign coming out of my mouth. I stay close to the truth in order to paint a picture of intimacy that is awe-inspiring without being scary, to hold something up to the boys that is at once an enormous, powerful responsibility, and also the most ordinary thing in the world. The truth is something that is both a toddler on her mother's lap and the passionate embrace of newlyweds.

I'm sure my mom knew this, too. As deep as her love ran for me, she knew that "fifteen minutes" wasn't the best answer to my question. But that certainly was the very best she could do.

Sharon Laidlaw-Almaguer is a mother, writer, teacher, and full-time mentor to new teachers. She shares insights and builds a community of educators through her blog, teachermentor.org. Her own mentors are the teachers she coaches, her two sons, and her wife.

Stay a While Longer, Mama

by Kristin Vanderhey Shaw

It's 11:48 PM on a Sunday night, and the phone rings shrilly. Some unimportant TV movie is playing and I nearly jump out of bed from the unexpected sound. At first, all I hear is silence, and I start to hang up the phone. Then I'm stopped cold when I hear a ragged breath and the sound of my name. The voice is familiar, but it's shrouded in a sob, echoing in my head like a gong.

"Kristin. It's Mom. Grandma died."

"What? What? What," I repeat until the phone drops from my hand.

My boyfriend picks up the phone from the floor and speaks to my mother in low voices until I recover, and hands the phone back to me. I grip it so hard my knuckles would hurt if I could feel something.

"Mom, it's me," I say, shaking with sobs so violent I can barely take a breath. "I'll meet you in Fort Lauderdale tomorrow. I love you."

"I have to call Tracey," she says, hoarse and incoherent.

"I'll do it, Mom. I'll call her." She doesn't protest. It's a physical effort to put the phone down and I continue to hold it in my hands for a few moments, as though I could hold my mother through the phone.

Picking up the phone again, I call my little sister. It's after midnight, and I know she's sleeping, and surely my baby niece is sleeping as well, but I know she wouldn't want me to wait until morning. She answers the phone at three rings and I am paralyzed with anguish.

Taking a deep breath, I say, "Trace, I just talked to Mom. Grandma died this morning."

"No," my sister wails into the phone. The sound permeates every cell of my body as we cry together. When we hang up, I lie down on my bed and stare at the ceiling. The tears won't stop leaking from my swollen eyes and I don't bother to wipe them away.

It is the next morning and I am on a plane to Florida. Slouching in my standard-issue coach seat, I turn to the window and let the tears come; I'm pretty sure someone is sitting beside me but I don't even know if it's a man or woman. For once, I don't read the in-flight magazine or the catalog of unnecessary items, dreaming about the house I would furnish with prism gazing balls in the garden, towel warmers for the bathrooms, and huge, fluffy dog beds for the family room. Arriving at the airport, my mother and cousin meet me at baggage claim. Did I check my bag? I can't remember. I look around the terminal and see anxious boyfriends waiting with flowers, grandchildren playing on the divider ropes, and chauffeurs looking bored, holding signs for people they have never met. Falling into my mother's arms, my tears renew themselves, and people stare in curiosity. All I notice is my mother's grief, so raw and fresh and overwhelming.

At the funeral home, my mother asks me if I want to see my grandmother's body. I say yes, and I walk into the room and I'm shocked that my beloved grandmother's body is in a white cardboard box. It's as though we're packing her for a move. In fact, we are, in a way. Her will specified that she was to be cremated, and I know her spirit is already gone.

I touch her face with my fingertips and feel the cool silkiness of her cheek. I remember how she would hold my hand and I would marvel at her soft skin at eighty-three years old. When she would hug me, her cheeks against mine were as soft as folds of satin. Now, her eyes are closed and she looks sad to me, somehow. Not at peace, like I hoped she would.

I remember playing cards with her and painting her fingernails. I remember her close-mouthed smile – she hated to show her teeth – and her strong voice. I smooth her hair at the top of her forehead and let a tear fall on her shoulder. I hate to see her like this, yet I don't want to let her go. I know that this image will haunt me for the rest of my life.

"*Io te amo molto*," my mother says for the last time. "I love you very much, mom."

I hear her choke back a sob again as I take her in my arms. I feel like the mother as she cries on my shoulder. In this very moment I know that I have closed the book on my childhood for good, finally and mournfully, at twenty-nine. Then we close the box and walk out of the room, my mother leaning on me heavily, to finish making the arrangements.

Before my grandmother died, my mother and I spoke on the phone a couple of times a week, tops. We checked in, and talked here and there. After my grandmother's death, I start calling my mother every day. Subconsciously, I am filling the void. Once, I travel to San Francisco on a business meeting, and I forget to call my mother when I land. When I finally reach her, hours later, she is crying.

"I thought something had happened to you," she said, through her tears. "I can't lose you."

And as we talk more and more as the weeks and months go by, we become closer. Left behind are my childhood conversations about mundane things; I have taken on the role of adult daughter and friend.

It's my wedding day, and I'm going through my things to find all the props I'll need. Dress – check. Veil – check. Shoes – check. Wedding band – there it is. A slender white-gold band with tiny diamonds cradled within, rests on my palm, winking at me. This ring means more to me than anything else; Gram gave it to me at Christmas, two weeks before she died.

"I want you to have this," she had said. "This was the first ring your grandfather bought me when I was nineteen. In 1935, he paid a dollar a week for it until it was paid off. And we didn't have two dimes to rub together in those days."

That was one of her favorite sayings. Not to mention the incendiary phrases she taught me in Italian that drove my mother crazy. I was the only kid in a wide radius of my Indiana neighborhood that could – and did – tell the boys that I was going to break their face in *Italiano*. I smile at the memory.

That same day, she had showed me where she was hiding the crocheted blanket she had almost finished for my first-born child. I wasn't married yet, and she was making baby blankets. Maybe she knew that she wouldn't be here to give it to me when I had a baby.

As I dress, I wear the band on my right hand and feel her presence in the room. Walking up the long sidewalk to the Southern manor where I'm about to be married, I look for her sitting on the white folding chairs and feel the sting of her absence. I realize that one of the most important people in my life isn't there and I feel suddenly sad, jarring me out of my wedding-day happiness. I think of my mother, and how much she must miss her, too.

As the pastor begins to speak at the beginning of the ceremony, a dragonfly lands on the back of my dress. I don't feel or see it, at first. I turn to look at my mother, her eyes shining brightly, and I notice the dragonfly's long body from the corner of my eye. It stays on my dress for the entire twenty-minute service, lightly fluttering its wings. As I turn to my new husband, it floats away. My mother tells me she is sure that it's Gram's spirit watching over me, and I can see the look of love and still-fresh grief in her eyes when she tells me so. But she feels better somehow, she says.

It is when I am going through a divorce, ten years later, that I see my mother's gossamer fragility and steely strength, hand in hand. She is devastated that I am in pain, and she listens to me beg for strength on the other end of the phone, dissolved by tears, hundreds of miles away. Yet she stands up and tells me that I will survive this. She reminds me to remember the happy things in my life. She swears under her breath and calls my soon-to-be ex-husband every bad name in the book in both English and Italian.

And later still, when I remarry and have a child of my own, I realize that I have started bossing my mother around as though I am smarter than she is. I suffer from postpartum anxiety, and in the midst of the struggling, I forget that my mother raised two daughters already, and quite well, thank you. And yet, nothing she does seems to be right when it comes to my son.

"Why are you holding him like that? He doesn't like that."

"Please keep your eye on him."

"Swaddle him like this, not like that."

I'm not sure why I believe that I am God's gift to mothering and that she doesn't have any idea what she's doing.

My mother and I take a drive to run some errands while I am visiting her in Florida. I am once again telling her what to do and how to do it, and suddenly I stop. I put my hand on hers as she drives and I say, "Why do I do that?"

"Do what?" she asks.

"Tell you what to do as if you are a child," I say. I am sheepish.

She opens her mouth and a laugh peals out like a bell. "I did the same to my mother, too," she says.

We laugh together as I remember my mother telling her mother, "Ma, get up. We're going to the store. No, you can't stay home. Get your clothes on or you're going in your nightgown."

I am my mother, in so many ways. And it's not all bad.

The time is racing by and I feel as though I want to bottle every second. I know from experience that when one has a child, someone is going to give you that "enjoy every moment" advice. Everyone knows that you can't possibly do that, but you try, because they're little for such a short period of time. They are growing so fast. It seems that you blink, and he is bigger. She is growing out of her shoes. He is learning a new skill. She no longer says, "Pick you up" or "I yuv you," and you didn't get a chance to record it because it happened so fast and you thought that you had plenty of time.

It's only recently that I realized that this ubiquitous phrase also applies to mothers. As in the mother who raised me, and sent me to college, and still loves me as fiercely as ever. The same one who rushed me to the hospital countless times for asthma attacks and pneumonia. The one who cried for me when I was sad and cheered for me when I was happy. The one who loved me enough to give me rules and guidelines. The one I talk to nearly every day.

I try not to speculate on how many years I have left with her. The thought of losing her gives me a feeling of dropping down the deepest, darkest well imaginable. I have so much to ask her, and I sometimes feel as though I'm dashing to catch up.

I have started to ask my mother more and more questions – the questions I wish I had asked my grandmother when she was alive. What were you like as a child? What was your house like? How did you feel about your parents? What were your greatest accomplishments? Do you have any regrets? How do you make that pie we love so much? Were you as worried about me as a baby as I am about my son? What does it feel like to be a grandparent?

I look to my left, and there is my son, five years old going on twenty. He has grown an inch and a half in the last two months and has outgrown all of his shoes. He is, and will always be, my baby.

To my right is my mother, now sixty-nine. I soak in all of her stories and her company, scrambling to stuff as much time as I can with her when I see her. It's like trying to pin a wave to the sand with a toothpick. And I am, and will always be, her baby.

And yet, I try. I remind myself that I will miss every idiosyncrasy when she is gone, someday. Every day, I pray that it is not soon. Every day, my heart beats a little faster when my mother calls me on the phone. And every day, I look forward to her voice.

Stay a while longer, mama. I will need you forever.

Kristin Shaw is a freelance writer, 2014 BlogHer Voice of the Year, 2013 Babble 100 blog, and co-producer of the Listen to Your Mother show in Austin, where she is the mother of a mini-Texan. Her work has been featured at Huffington Post; Washington Post; Brain, Child; the Erma Bombeck Workshop; In The Powder Room; and Scary Mommy, among others. Shaw is also a consultant in the aviation industry and Director of Social Media for Airport Improvement magazine.

Catching Bullets
by Robyn Rasberry

It was one of those moments that could have turned terribly tragic. She's not frail, but there was no way her seven-year-old body could have withstood the weight of the dresser that was tipping to land square on top of her. It was a moment I dread and fear as a parent. One that keeps me awake, alert, and accused of hovering.

Being raised by a nurse and a firefighter, I was afforded the privilege of awareness. My awareness came in the form of storytelling. Graphic storytelling. I knew at a painfully young age that sometimes grandparents back over their grandbabies in the driveway. Sometimes TV consoles tip over onto toddlers. Sometimes children pull down hot pans from the stove, onto their skin. Sometimes young siblings hide in the closet to play with the matches they found outside.

I learned that Tragedy happens. The vein of the stories was never laced with judgment or blame. I was taught that Tragedy cannot be obliterated by attentive parenting. I was taught to fear the happenstance of the universe. It is unpredictable and undiscriminating.

"Bad things happen," my dad would tell me. "All you can do is try to be prepared."

Preparation was the name of the game. It wasn't the underground/canned goods preparation for End Times. It was a mental and emotional preparedness. The preparation training usually came in the form of slogans and cliché mantras.

"Don't burn your bridges," dad would say. This was meant to prepare me for the moments in my life when Tragedy would strike, leaving me needing the assistance of others. You see, if I piss everyone off, they won't want to help me when I need it most.

"A meal is a meat, a starch, and a green thing," my mother would always recite. This was meant to help me avoid the Tragedy of heart disease and ailments worthy of hospitalization.

The slogans ranged from playful to sinister. Never leave the handle of the pan hanging over the stove edge. Never leave a child in the bathtub alone. Never drive without shoes. Never answer the front door when you're alone. Always know your exits in a room. And the one I remember most clearly, take the bullet. This was meant to guide me in an abduction situation. If I'm ever held at gunpoint and forced into a car with a stranger, it's best to fight and possibly take a bullet. A death in the street is better than the unknown fate that awaits after the car ride. A kidnapper, you see, probably wouldn't take a girl if she was wounded. There are worse things than death, I was told.

These were the signposts of my awareness education. I understood far better than my peers that Tragedy happens all the time. I felt comforted by my knowledge, and I tried to shepherd my poor, naïve playmates whose parents weren't as knowledgeable of the world. It wasn't until I was breaching my teens that I recognized my inability to cope with the kind of imagery I was handed.

In raising my own daughter, I have tried to instill a healthy amount of fear of Tragedy, without the gory details. I have handed down guidance and warnings through generalities, hoping her outlook would be one of precautionary awareness without the burden of paranoia. My goal is to grow a proactive child whose natural awareness would negate the need for cited examples of past Tragedy. I was hoping to avoid telling the stories with gruesome outcomes, like when heavy furniture accidentally tips over on soft and yielding children.

I was buzzing around in the morning light of our apartment, readying myself for a day off with my daughter. I zipped into her room, my hands gripped around my coffee mug and the bits of paper I was moving from one place to the next.

"Go ahead and get your fashion for the day so we can go get pancakes," I told her. I turned on my heels and headed to get myself dressed.

She was simply beaming at the idea of stuffing those chocolate chip pancakes in her face. It was a weekly routine we had gotten into, having a Mom-Daughter-Pancake-Date. She would pick her favorite fashion for the occasion.

She calls her clothing "fashion," not because each piece is anything unique, but because of the way she arranges and layers and coordinates her outfits. Her sense of style is well beyond her years. She takes pride in the combinations and silhouettes she creates while rummaging through her very own four-drawer dresser.

It must have been like a tower of treasures to her. It stood right at her chin, adorned with her breakable knick-knacks deemed too precious to join her other toys.

I heard her lamp hit the floor first. I was only five or six steps away in the other room.

"Bela," I called. My voice was pointed and sharp. I could hear the seriousness stain my tone.

The only sound that answered was her music box hitting the floor.

"Bela! Bela!"

She didn't answer. I continued saying her name as I turned back toward her room.

I don't remember what happened to the things in my hands. I don't remember the one or two seconds it took for me to understand the chaos I was looking at in her room. Every item atop her dresser was now debris, scattered around her. The four drawers of the dresser had all rolled open, scattering the contents. The full weight of the dresser was only about six inches away from her tiny body on the floor. In that moment she seemed so small. I caught a glimpse of her frame, tucking into a tight ball, right before disappearing under the falling dresser.

I don't remember doing it, but I threw as much of myself as I could into the chaos. The weight of the dresser pressed my arms into her body, frozen and silent. I couldn't lift the dresser any higher than I had caught it.

"Bela. I'm here. It's okay. Can you move, baby?"

"I'm okay. I'm okay."

She was able to pull herself out from under the dresser, pushing aside all the pieces of her prized possessions. She tucked herself close to me, as I let the

weight of the dresser hit the floor. I turned to her and
wrapped around her with every inch of my body. I've never
held anything so closely.

I could feel both of us trembling through the
remnants of fear and adrenaline. I didn't let go while taking
inventory.

"Are you hurt?"

"I'm okay. I promise."

"Did anything hit you?"

"Only a little. I'm okay."

Bela has never been comfortable communicating
pain. I'm not sure what the adults in her life have done to
cause her such hesitation, but she has always seemed to
fear punishment for her injuries. As though being hurt isn't
enough. This time was no different.

I took her out of her room, away from the visual
reminder of Tragedy's attempt on us that morning. I
inspected closely each "little bump" she reported. A few of
the heavier things had hit her on the way down, but had not
hit anything vital.

"Am I in trouble?" she asked, timidly.

"Absolutely not. You didn't do anything wrong.
That wasn't your fault."

"But I was trying to open the drawer. I pulled too
hard."

I held her and continued insisting. I convinced her
with patient and soft persistence until she finally let her
muscles relax into mine. We sat and held each other until
our tremors subsided. As soon as they did, I knew I had to
reset her brain. I didn't want the heavy threat in the air to

be her lasting emotional impression. I didn't want my tears to be the thing that lingered in her mind.

"Okay, supergirl, let's go get you some chocolate chip pancakes." My tone was the permission she needed to bounce out of and past her fear.

We spent the rest of the day as playfully as we could. I quietly relayed the incident to the other adults in her life, and she loudly required me to get the dresser out of her room.

I didn't get questions from my parents. There was no blame. There was no, "Why didn't you anchor the dresser?" or "Why weren't you paying closer attention?" They understood, as they always have, that Tragedy doesn't only choose the warranted. The first and only thing they said was, "Thank God she's okay. Thank God you got there in time."

I don't believe there is a God to thank, though I have no other force to which I assign reason. I am usually grounded in my understanding of the universe, even if it is quite limited. I know the laws of physics made that dresser come down. It's the simple equation of weight and force that is the culprit, not the mysterious or magical temperament of Tragedy.

I must admit, though, the moment has prompted my mind to wander. Was it likely the dresser would fall? No. Was it, in truth, a result of neglect? Probably not. What then? Was it coincidence? Chance? Fate?

What if I hadn't been close enough to catch it? What if the moment had been one of those life-altering ones instead of just the footnote of our weekend?

Would a slogan have helped? Never pull on heavy furniture. Always get up and run instead of tucking into a ball underneath the heavy furniture that's falling on top of you. Never leave my side. Ever.

I understand now that my parents sang the slogans to me because they simply don't know why Tragedy happens. They recite their preventative mantras in the hope that one reminder might someday be enough to help me escape pain or suffering. It's the one proactive thing they can do to combat the unpredictable and undiscriminating.

I don't know why bad things happen. I don't know why good people suffer. I don't know what "good" really means. I don't know what evil actually is, and I don't know the precise meaning of luck. I don't know why accidents happen or how Tragedy chooses its victims. I don't know why I was there in time and why other parents weren't.

These are my mantras. These are the slogans I keep, tucked at the back of my tongue. I don't share them with Bela often. Instead, I tell her that I love her. I tell her that I want her to be the best Bela she can, so that she can rule her world, in whatever form it comes. I tell her to be brave and wise. I tell her that her boldness is more valuable than her fear. I tell her that her perfection is her flaws. I tell her that growth sometimes hurts and that pain is inevitable. I tell her she is strong and capable, and I want her to believe it. I want her to believe that she can handle the happenstance of the universe because I won't always be there hovering. I won't always be able to catch the dresser.

Robyn lives in Texas with her daughter, Bela, her husband, Ryan, and her Chihuahua, Emma. When she isn't teaching 8th grade English or acting as Managing Editor of Robyn Lane Books, she is writing, filming, or singing loudly in the car. Robyn's work is also published on GreatMomentsinParenting.com and in <u>Listen to Your Mother</u>.

My Son Hits Like a Girl
by Lane Buckman

My mother was an athlete. She played baseball so well that she was scouted by a major league team, who thought the Jo Young they kept hearing about was a Joseph, not a Joan. The scout told her coach it was a damned shame she wasn't a boy because he would have recruited the shortstop phenom, who could hit a homerun from a crouched position, and play catcher like she was Johnny Bench.

She was a dancer, too. She was graceful, and coordinated, and could pick up and repeat complex choreography like it was just banging a drum.

She outran, out-played, and even out-boxed every boy in her Army Base-adjacent neighborhood. Maybe more than all that, she was the special kind of all-around athlete, who knows how to get the best out of the people around her. She coached misfits to victory on a regular basis, with a blend of practice, patience, and intelligence.

And then she had me. Bless her heart.

I tried to come into this world sideways, and that's probably how I'll go out of it because I am the least coordinated, least athletic, least physically intelligent person in my family. There was that time in 9th grade, when I broke my wrist trying to spike a volleyball. Two days later, I was in my backyard, trying to dance like Simon LeBon, when I broke my ankle. Two days after that, I was hopping for my crutches, and dislocated my knee, ending up in a wheelchair and in detention for nearly running over a nun in the school hallway. My chair was being pushed, obviously, because with the broken wrist, I could really only wheel myself in circles.

My mother laughed. She'd had fifteen years to get used me at that point. She was used to the broken bones and sprains, the pulled muscles, the scrapes, cuts, bruises, and the concussions and head wounds that I brought home for her to nurse, from my everyday interactions with the world. She was also an incredible nurse. Another skill that skipped my generation.

Once, my mother told me she'd been afraid she wouldn't know what to do with a girl. As rough and tumble as she had been, she was afraid she couldn't help a girl find her value. After all, the things that she thought made her the most valuable were stereotypically masculine. What would she do if she had a child who loved baby dolls and pink?

Exactly what she did, I guess, because every inch of my soul was born to Girl. If girl can be a verb, I did it. I girled so hard. Pink, sparkles, lace, fluff, dolls, glass slippers, pageants, and plays were my world. If it didn't already have some glitter on it, I could fix that. I would happily have put lipstick on a pig. Or a dog. My poor dog.

My mother might not have known what to do with all that, but it never showed. She bought me ruffles and patent leather, took me to have my hair done, bought me a vanity table and encouraged my interests. As much as I girled, she momed. She coached. She was the consummate coach, finding what I was good at, and bringing that forward, while working to build the muscles I lacked.

She gave up on my sports muscles by the time I was thirteen. At the time of my retirement from junior high softball, my most spectacular play had been accidentally catching a pop fly, then sitting down on 3rd base to block a

runner because I couldn't remember what else I was
supposed to do with the ball. I will never forget the look
on her face with that one.

In spite of my athletic inabilities, she never gave up
on coaching me as her daughter. Of course I couldn't
appreciate the effort. I was a normal kid, who believed my
parents were only set on this earth to ruin my life. Or,
RUIN MY LIFE, as I liked to wail it. It wasn't until I had
my baby that I started to understand the mental fortitude,
the practice, patience, and intelligence it takes to raise a
child, to coach a child.

I had a boy. I have a boy. And my boy is more
coordinated, more naturally talented physically, more
aware of his body and space than his father and I put
together. When he was three, he could hit a pitched ball.
He just innately understood what it took to make a
connection between body, bat, and ball, and he could drive
a hit longways across our backyard. I have video for any
unbelievers.

I had no idea what to do with my glorious creature.
I knew books and writing, acting and fashion, music and lip
gloss, and while all those things have their places in the
world, outside the inherent drama of sports, they have no
play on the greens, or the pitches, or the fields of dreams.
Sure, David Beckham wears guy liner, but not while he's
kicking balls around.

What I learned from my mother, my coach, is that a
good mother isn't layering her interests onto her child.
Being a good mother isn't about self-fulfillment. It isn't
about doing what you like best, or even what comes
naturally to you. It isn't forcing flat feet into soccer boots.

It is about finding what comes naturally to your
child and stretching, strengthening, and refining those

muscles. It's about becoming a student of your child's nature and nurturing the best in him, to coach that maximum potential out of him. It is about practice, patience, and intelligence. Your practice. Your patience. Your intelligence.

My mother had no idea what to do with her glorious creature, so she studied me. She set herself to learning me. She became an expert in Lane, then she found the other coaches who could draw the best out of me.

She found places where I could excel. There were college level literary courses, special trips to the museums and theatre, charm schools, and talent agents, and voice lessons, and fashion shows. There were also, at my insistence, the failed ice skating lessons, tennis lessons, dance lessons, and gymnastics. As I fell, tripped, and concussed myself out of each of those, she was there to drive me to the emergency room, and gently direct me toward my natural talents.

She helped me cultivate my own style with endless applause, and she regarded my athletic failures with so much love, that even though I never got to enjoy the thrill of victory, I have never been afraid of, or embarrassed by defeat. Her passion for my well-being means that I can enjoy a loss as much as anyone has ever loved winning. She taught me that losing the game isn't failure. Failure is being afraid to play.

She held me to a standard, but that standard was what she had ascertained to be my best. I was never compared to anyone else. She taught me to compete against my own records, to strive against my own personal victories, and to always reach, stretch, and want for more.

When it comes to coaching my own child, I am fortunate. My son loves to read as much as he loves to run. He'll challenge you to a game of chess as quickly as he'll jump into a game of dodge ball. That makes it easier for me on the sidelines. I can find easy ways to relate.

I am also fortunate that when it comes to cultivating his natural prowess at sports, he has my mom.

She finally got that boy to play catch with, and when he started playing Coach Pitch baseball, two years ago, it was my mother who sat and watched his practice, studying his stance, his swing, and his body language. It was my mother who took what was naturally good and taught him how to make it great.

When he went back to his batting practice, his coaches did that thing you only ever see in the movies. Hats came off. Eyes went wide. Heads started bobbing.

"Son," his coach called to him, "son, who taught you that? Your dad?"

My boy broke into a grin. "My grandma taught me!"

My son hits like a girl. Like a seventy-three year old girl. His coach asked for an introduction.

Sixty years later, coaches are still mistaking my mother's amazing abilities for a man's. But I'm here to tell you that there is no coach alive like my mighty Jo Young, whose patience, practice, and intelligence showed me that a good mother can cultivate an artist as easily as an athlete.

Lane Buckman is a writer, and the co-owner of Robyn Lane Books. She lives in Dallas, Texas with her family and their silly-looking dog, Hoo. When she isn't being chased around the house by Booger-Finger, the Fart Monster, or the dog, she is generally working on promoting RLB authors, writing, editing, reading, or painting. In her free time, she has a day job in finance.

www.ingramcontent.com/pod-product-compliance
Lightning Source LLC
Chambersburg PA
CBHW071005120726
47910CB00004B/1386